Emotional Intelligence and Empath Mastery

A Complete Guide for Self Healing & Discovery, Increasing Self Discipline, Social Skills, Cognitive Behavioral Therapy, NLP, Persuasion & More.

By Ewan Miller

"Emotional Intelligence and Empath Mastery: A Complete Guide for Self Healing & Discovery, Increasing Self Discipline, Social Skills, Cognitive Behavioral Therapy, NLP, Persuasion & More." Written by "Ewan Miller".

Emotional Intelligence and Empath Mastery is a bundle of the books "Emotional Intelligence - Life Mastery", & "Guided Self-Healing and Mindfulness Meditations Bundle".

Hope You Enjoy!

Emotional Intelligence – Life Mastery

Practical Self-Development Guide for Success in Business and Your Personal Life-Improve Your Social Skills, NLP, EQ, Relationship Building, CBT & Self Discipline.

By Ewan Miller

Table of Contents

Emotional Intelligence – Life Mastery
Table of Contents
Introduction
Chapter 1: Understanding Emotional Intelligence

    Emotional intelligence versus intelligence quotient
    Emotional intelligence versus social intelligence
    Emotional intelligence in psychology
    A brief history of emotional intelligence
    Other research and studies on emotional intelligence
    Emotional intelligence framework
    High and low emotional intelligence
    Why developing emotional intelligence is crucial
    Self and relationship management
    Emotional intelligence in the workplace
    Emotional intelligence and relationships

Chapter 2: The Application of Emotional Intelligence

    Handling Impulses
    Handling difficulties and setbacks
    Handling stress and anxiety
    In the workplace
    Coping with trauma
    Coping with reactions

Chapter 3: Recognizing Emotions

    Envy
    Worry or nervousness
    Anger or aggravation
    Dislike
    Disappointment or unhappiness

Chapter 4: Improving Emotional Intelligence

    Emotional intelligence in the relationship
    Body language
    Active listening
    Mindfulness and relaxation techniques

Chapter 5: Emotional Intelligence and Leadership

    Good leadership
    Adaptation
    Leadership and performance
    The six styles of leadership
    How to improve
    The five components of emotional intelligence in leadership
    Social skills

Conclusion

Empath – A Complete Healing Guide

Self-Discovery, Coping Strategies, Survival Techniques for Highly Sensitive People. Dealing with the Effects of Empathy and how to develop to Enhance Your Life NOW!

By Ewan Miller

Table of Contents

Introduction

Chapter 1: What is an Empath?

    Are You Empathic or an Empath?
    How Does It Feel to Be an Empath?
    Most Common Traits of Empaths
    Born Empaths vs. Learned Empaths
    Are You an Empath? QUIZ

Chapter 2: The Empath's Peace of Mind and What Hinders It

    Common Problems as an Empath
    The Narcissist and the Empath

What Are "Energy Vampires"?
Downsides to Being a Powerful Empath

Chapter 3: The Gift of Being an Empath

The Benefits of Being an Empath
Self-Awareness and the Awareness of Others
Healing and Helping Others
Possible Professions to Help You Thrive in Life as an Empath

Chapter 4: Healing and Balancing Tools for the Empath

What Are Spiritual Healing Tools and How to Use Them
Energy Clearing for the Self and Others
Awareness and Mindfulness Practices
Steps to a Grounding and Balancing Meditation

Chapter 5: How to Keep Unwanted Energy from Influencing You as an Empath

When Other People Are Negative: Ways to Protect Yourself
Grounding: Before and After
Communicating Boundaries

Chapter 6: Quality Space and Time

Why You Should Limit Time with Other People or Groups
Space and Time for Reflection and Rejuvenation
Relationships and the Empath

Chapter 7: How to Avoid Empathic Burnout

Guidelines for Maintaining Balance and Stability
Applications to Aid You in Times of Stress or Burnout

Conclusion

Introduction

If you were looking for a book on emotional intelligence that is highly practical and offers a guide for success in business and personal life than this is the right book. The book delves onto social skills, emotional quotient, relationship building, self-discipline and cognitive behavior therapy using simple to understand language. Using easy and relatable examples, the author introduces what constitutes emotional intelligence, why it differs from the intelligent quotient and offer ways of improving social skills at work and home using emotional intelligence. For this reason, this book is both a manual and a discussion of applicable emotional intelligence for beginners and seasoned individuals.

In uniformly spaced subtopics, the author guides the reader on how to apply emotional intelligence by handling impulses, managing setbacks, and handling stress and anxiety. The book walks the reader through applying emotional intelligence at the workplace, handling trauma, and coping with reactions. The reader is taken through ways of recognizing emotions especially the common and negative emotions at the workplace. Some of the common and negative emotions explored are anger, nervousness, unhappiness, and dislike. Emotionally intelligence is also applied in relationships and in leadership and the reader is exposed to how emotional intelligence affects leadership and relationships as well as how to enhance emotional intelligence.

Chapter 1: Understanding Emotional Intelligence

Emotional intelligence versus intelligence quotient

The individual ability to evaluate, identify, manage and express emotions is known as emotional intelligence. Persons with high emotional intelligence are likely to make efficient leaders and team players since they possess the ability to empathize, understand, and link with people around them. On the other hand, intelligent quotient evaluates academic abilities and identifies persons with mental challenges or persons with exceptional abilities. At the workplace, emotional intelligence is a widely accepted indicator of success to help acknowledge good team players, leaders, and independent workers.

In detail, intelligence quotient captures abilities such as fluid reasoning, knowledge of the world, spatial and visual processing, quantitative reasoning, and working memory and short-term memory. On the other hand, emotional intelligence captures the way of relating to others, identifying emotions, assessing how others feel, managing individual emotions, and perceiving how others feel as well as employing emotions to enable social communication. Initially, intelligence quotient was seen as the fundamental determinant of success as persons deemed to have high intelligence quotient were seen as destined for accomplishments. All this led to a debate about whether intelligence is a product of the environment or gene factors.

With time critics started to acknowledge that high intelligence is not a guarantee for accomplishment in life. Additionally, intelligence quotient alone could not capture the full spectra of human abilities and knowledge. When it comes to academic achievement intelligent quotients is still accepted as a critical element of success. Persons with high intelligent quotients are likely to excel in school and earn more money as well as having a healthier life. Contemporary experts acknowledge that intelligent quotient is not the only determinate of success in life. Against this backdrop, the intelligent quotient is seen as integral of an intricate array of influences that include emotional intelligence.

Equally important is that the concept of emotional intelligence has had a significant impact in a number of areas especially the business domain. Most organizations now demand emotional intelligence training and employ emotional quotient tests as integral to the hiring process. Persons with effective leaders tend to exhibit high emotional intelligent insinuating that a high emotional quotient is a critical component of business leadership and management.

An illustration can be when you take an insurance company that realizes that emotional intelligence can play a critical role in the success of sales. It then emerges that sales agents that rank lower on emotional intelligence abilities such as empathy, self-confidence, and initiative tend to sell an average premium of $45, 000 compared to those agents that rank high on emotional intelligence scores that sell an average of $105, 000.

Additionally, emotional abilities can be used to impact the choices that consumers make when faced with buying decisions. Most people prefer to deal with an individual that they trust and like compared to someone they do not and this implies paying more for an inferior product.

Indeed emotional intelligence can be learned. Some of the ways that emotional intelligence can be imparted are through character education, encouraging people to think about how others are feeling, modeling positive behaviors, and discovering ways to be more empathetic toward others. Like any other form of coaching, the candidate for training should be willing to gain knowledge and practice it. A person seeking to enhance his or her emotional intelligence levels should first do a self-evaluation of weaknesses that relate to emotional intelligence and then do more evaluation using the guideline of an expert. When coaching someone on emotional intelligence, it should be implemented gradually and adjusted to the individual needs of the candidate.

In overall, both intelligent quotient and emotional quotient play critical roles in impacting the overall success of an individual including wellness, health, and happiness. Learning to improve the skills in weak areas to more than average is important than just focusing on the gifted areas. The reason for this argument is that as an individual, your whole is more important than the specific strengths. Think of it this way, you are a highly intelligent worker but unable to handle disappointments which compromise your overall productivity. Alternatively, think yourself as a highly emotionally stable person and have the unique ability to engage others but have difficulties learning new technologies and systems at the workplace which ends up affecting your overall productivity. Ideally, having a balance of the intelligent quotient and emotional quotient is highly beneficial. Fortunately, there are proven methods to help work on your weak areas to make you whole.

Exercise

a. As part of the hiring team looking for a replacement of an Information Technology Officer at your company, you only managed to shortlist two candidates where one of the candidates is a sharp person with respect to academic accomplishments but appears temperamental. The other is average in academics but appears emotionally stable and warm to engage. How would you handle the hiring process to end up with the most suitable candidate for your organization?

b. Get any episode of Bing Bang Theory TV series and make a first impression of Sheldon Cooper character. Assume that only observation is enough to judge an individual, would you hire Sheldon Cooper? Why and Why not?

Emotional intelligence versus social intelligence

Emotional intelligence relates to the present and emotions manifesting. For instance, a mother knows how the baby is feeling. The mother knows if the baby is sad or hungry. Alternatively, think of a shy and scared teenager at a party. You managed to perceive this because you have emotional quotient applied appropriately. On the other hand, social intelligence concerns more about the future as you are relying on present knowledge to enhance the future by looking for the best pathway for you. For instance, a worker in an organization that looks for a different way to disagree with the boss on the new measures being implemented.

In this manner, social intelligence concerns comprehending the personalities and corresponding behaviors of people to understand how to best get along. The intent of social intelligence is to precipitate positive outcomes from interactions between people. On the other hand, emotional intelligence concerns helping an individual become aware of his emotional status and manage it to make him or her more relatable. Taking all this into account, emotional intelligence is a prerequisite of social intelligence where social intelligence is the derivative of the former. Simply put, without a person having requisite emotional intelligence levels he or she is likely to perform poorly in social interactions. Think of Sheldon Cooper in the TV series Big Bang Theory.

The further explanation includes acknowledging that social intelligence is when emotional intelligence is applied in a group setting making everyone comfortable, accommodative and civil. For this reason, social intelligence has evolved to enable us to survive. Think of survival and accomplishment at your career requires more than just good grades. For instance, you might be highly qualified but respond poorly to questions seeking to ascertain your emotional stability. In other terms reacting rudely at your interviewers constitutes a signal that you have low social intelligence level. Lack of manifesting requisite social intelligence can increase the risk of losing jobs, opportunities or friendship.

An illustration of social intelligence may be the case of Richard who is a stereotypical office employee. Richard is socially intelligent enough to comprehend that his boss is offended at casual bad news. For this reason, Richard understands that it is socially intelligent to phrase negative news in a way that begins with positive aspects of the news to avoid triggering an emotional reaction from his boss. On the other hand, Richard understands that if he shares the news with Juliet that she will casually share it and does not think about the consequences of her actions when spreading the news. Against this backdrop, Richard employs socially intelligent and avoids telling Juliet to save when the news is wholly positive.

Additionally, Richard employs emotional intelligence in conference meetings. Now assume that everything is going well at his Tuesday meeting but suddenly he notices facial expressions on Juliet that indicates that she is feeling irked and agitated. Richard then adjusts the delivery and notices that Juliet is now calm and settled with the suggested project but remains mum. It is through emotional intelligent that Richard manages to seek the opinion of Juliet on the project. Juliet provides her opinion and this helps to constructively move the project forward as they both reach a consensus. The above two illustrations demonstrate the functional difference between emotional intelligence and social intelligence.

For further emphasis, emotional intelligence requires certain competencies that include the following; self-awareness that addresses emotional awareness, self-confidence and self-assessment. Emotional intelligence also requires one to possess self-regulation that includes adaptability, innovativeness, self-control, conscientiousness, and trustworthiness. The other component of emotional intelligence includes self-motivation that covers commitment, drive, initiative, and optimism. Emotional intelligence requires one to be exhibit social awareness that addresses service orientation, empathy, leveraging diversity, developing others, and political awareness. Finally, emotional intelligence requires exhibiting social skills that include leadership, communication, conflict management, change management, and cooperation. All these are the comprehensive areas of emotional intelligence training that one needs.

Finally, social intelligence concerns the competence that helps an individual relationship with others. Social intelligence can be split into relationship-management and social-awareness. All these sub-concepts can be studied differently from the main concept, social intelligence that has been dubbed emotional and social intelligence. Rightly, social intelligence is a derivative of emotional intelligence. In this manner, social intelligence extends emotional intelligence. The purpose of this emphasis is to enable trainers and candidates to understand what should precede the other. Emotional intelligence coaching should precede social intelligence training. In simplest terms, you have to understand and manage yourself before you can positively engage other people.

Exercise

a. How can you enhance your social intelligence at school or workplace?

b. Think of a politician that has difficulties relating with others and suggest five ways the politician can improve his or her social skills.

Emotional intelligence in psychology

Various researchers affirm the assertion that several personality disorders are mediated or moderated by the emotional intelligence of an individual. In the context of psychology, emotional intelligence concerns sets of skills to facilitate, acknowledge, comprehend, and manage emotions that allow the use of emotional knowledge to attain a higher adjustment as well as psychological wellbeing. By having a high emotional intelligence you are likely to have a positive frame of mind, are likely to redress your mood after adverse emotions as well as score lower on stress, anxiety, and depression.

Notably, the connection between emotional intelligence and psychology is supported by the realization that patients with several clinical disorders show deficits in emotional intelligence score. The assumption that we form here is that a low score in emotional intelligence suggests varied potency for clinical disorders. For instance, various studies assert that most attention deficit individuals show a deficit in any of these emotional competencies. The other assumption that we make here is that emotional intelligence competencies contribute to the development and maintenance of the attention deficit.

Patients with social anxiety show a strong correlation between the seriousness of the symptoms and the difficulty to sufficiently perceive emotions and employ them to facilitate their thinking.

Furthermore, individuals with pathological demand avoidance condition exhibit significantly lower scores in emotional understanding and management skills compared to the healthy control group participants. All these indicate that deficit deficits in emotional understanding and integration are integral in the phenomenology of panic disorder. Individuals with general anxiety disorder focus more on their emotions and have critical difficulties in addressing their negative moods. Persons with general anxiety disorder degree of symptoms are related to their difficulties to clearly differentiate between various emotional states. The implication of this assertion is that perceived incapacity to manage your individual emotions could be a susceptible factor in the development of generalized anxiety disorder.

Against this backdrop, challenges with managing emotional states are a critical indicator of potentiality for personality disorders. In some nonclinical subjects, pathological personality traits are linked to critical deficits in emotional intelligence such as schizotypal, psychopathic, and borderline traits. It can then be argued that the presence of personality disorders in patients with attention deficit can be linked to higher deficits in emotional intelligence.

Correspondingly, emotional intelligence is critical to developing a balanced life. Emotional intelligence is not restricted to only communicating with people. Emotional intelligence should be treated as an avenue to realize a balanced-life. Every aspect of life requires emotional intelligence. For instance, emotional intelligence impacts physical health which is the ability to care for our bodies. By managing the stress that has a significant effect on our wellness we are acknowledging the critical role of emotional intelligence. By being aware of our emotional state as well as our reactions to stress we can hope to handle stress and maintain good health.

Expectedly, emotional intelligence affects our mental well-being by impacting our outlook and attitude on life. Emotional intelligence can aid in alleviating anxiety and avoid depression and mood swings. With this in mind, a high level of emotional intelligence directly correlates to a positive attitude as well as a happier outlook on life. We are better at communicating our feelings in a more helpful manner through comprehending and handling our emotions. In this manner emotional intelligence impacts relationships. Through emotional intelligence, we manage to comprehend and relate to others that we have interactions with. It is through understanding feelings, needs, and reactions of those we care about that inform stronger and more satisfying relationships.

Similarly, emotional intelligence impacts conflict resolution. It is through discerning the emotions of other people that we learn to empathize with their views of the issue making it easier to resolve conflicts or avoid the conflicts before they fester. The ability to comprehend the needs and desires of other people increases our efficiency at negotiation. Emotional intelligence also impacts success as higher emotional intelligence assists us to be assertive effective internal motivators that can help lower procrastination, enhance self-confidence, and enhance our ability to concentrate on a goal. Emotional intelligence can enhance our potentiality for success by enabling us to build better networks of support, conquer challenges, and preserve with a more robust outlook. In overall our ability to delay gratification and take into consideration the long-run directly impacts our ability to succeed.

Unfortunately, emotional intelligence in psychology also has a negative side. The danger of emotional intelligence is that it is morally neutral implying that it depends on how one uses it. Emotional intelligence can be charged and used by an individual to attain ulterior motives at the expense of others. Emotional intelligence can be used as an Asperger in which the individual may not understand what others are feeling. Emotional intelligence in a psychopath makes the individual not to care what you are feeling even though the individual is aware. Lastly, a Machiavellian manipulates how you feel to accomplish selfish ends. For Asperger Syndrome think of Sheldon Cooper of the Big Bang Theory TV series. Finally, persons with a high level of deception are likely to be the dominant members in a group setting and make the others merely pawns in helping the leader accomplish selfish ends.

Exercise

a. In your own terms explain how emotional intelligence links with psychology?

b. Do you agree that emotional intelligence scores correlate with various clinical personality disorders? Why and why not?

c. Try to link the aspect of deception as increasing the likelihood of the deceptive individual being a leader/dominant member of a group. Explain using public figures or celebrities or TV characters.

A brief history of emotional intelligence

Emotional intelligence as a separate construct did not exist until 1953 where Dorothy Van Ghent observed in her book exploring the Pride and Prejudice English novel that most of Jane Austen characters in the book exhibited a high emotional quotient. A German psychoanalyst, Barbara Leuner in 1966 argued that the drug LSD could help women with low emotional intelligence and at that time Leuner held the view that low emotional intelligence arose due to early separation from mothers that led to more emotional problems compared to the control group. However, the first individual to state the term emotional intelligence in an English language source was Wayne Payne through the 1986 dissertation. Wayne applied the term widely in his dissertation suggesting that emotional awareness was a critical component to develop in children.

Accordingly, it is the psychologists Mayer and Salovey that aligned with contemporary usage of the theory of emotional intelligence by offering the first formulation of the concept and an illustration of how emotional intelligence can be evaluated in two journal articles in 1990. During this period of the early 1990s, the concept of intelligence quotient was widely acknowledged as the gold standard of excellence in life. Equally important is that during this period the debate largely dominated around whether intelligent quotient was wired in our genes or acquired from the environment through individual experience. It was until 1995 that Daniel Goleman as a science reporter discovered Mayer and Salovey's studies and started to feel motivated by the thinking that there could be a novel way of viewing the components of life achievement.

Identically to Mayer and Salovey, Goleman employed the term emotional intelligence to capture a wide spectrum of scientific findings that drew together separate subdomains of research. The work of Goleman also covered other related scientific developments like the field of neuroscience which at its infancy at the time explored how emotions are managed in the brain. When Goleman published his work dubbed Emotional Intelligence and why it can count more than intelligence quotient in 1995, it gained global attention. During this period, most health professionals had not come across the idea of emotional intelligence despite Mayer and Salovey's studies being out for five years. So popular was the concept of emotional intelligence that Goleman's works became the best seller and impacted the world in several ways.

Additionally, Goleman noted that he felt elevated by hearing that educators had embraced emotional intelligence in the form of what is known as social and emotional learning. At the time of the seminal works of Goleman premiering; only a few schools ran programs teaching emotional intelligence skills to students. UNESCO in 2002 began a global initiative to promote social and emotional learning by developing ten fundamental principles for operationalizing social-emotional learning to at least 140 countries' ministries of education. They have been a number of attempts to evaluate the impact of direct instruction on a person's ability to exhibit emotional intelligence. In overall, some studies have exhibited significant success in measuring emotional intelligence while the other studies critique if emotional intelligence merits as a valid construct.

Notably, Mayer, Goleman, and Salovey proposed the notion of emotional intelligence partly due to the recognition of the unfair hegemony that the evaluation of intelligent quotient enjoyed at the period. There is a likelihood that they knew of persons with high intelligence but were not regarded as successful. Think of how in the contemporary workplace words such as nerd and geek still elicit much admiration. In essence, these slang terms describe an individual that is socially inadequate. So far it is convincing to assert that emotional intelligence competencies will impact the productivity of an individual, especially in teamwork setups.

Lastly, commanding a huge intelligence quotient attributes does not guarantee a person a satisfying human relationship and inner peace. Instead, such qualities are widely exhibited in the case of persons that have high emotional intelligence as well. For instance, a high intelligence quotient may enable a person to get shortlisted for a dream job but without emotional intelligence, the candidate may fail to impress at the interview stage. The example given illustrates how emotional intelligence may enhance the likelihood of success of an individual. The conclusion should be that emotional intelligence and intelligence quotient complement each other.

Exercise

a. In your opinion, who made a significant impact in drawing the world attention to the concept of emotional intelligence?

b. Do you hold the view that emotional intelligence proponents appear to subtly degrade the criticality of intelligence quotient?

Other research and studies on emotional intelligence

Recent studies on emotional intelligence share insight into how general intelligence and emotional intelligence affect student's academic and social abilities. From recent studies, it emerged that both general mental ability and emotional intelligence have an effect on the academic and social performance of students in college. However, general mental ability played a significant role in predicting academic performance compared to emotional intelligence. Another interesting discovery is that only emotional intelligence, as opposed to general mental ability, was related to the quality of social interactions with peers. We can argue that emotional interaction is required to enable you to work with others and indeed work with the public that prioritizes how you handled them compared to how smart you are. From these assertions, possessing more than average of emotional intelligence and intelligence quotient increases the likelihood of an individual excelling in school and at the workplace.

Additionally, recent research on emotional intelligence explored the individuals with schizophrenia if they exhibit impaired emotional intelligence in comparison to a control group and seeks to pinpoint the exact emotional intelligence areas of weakness in the case that the assertion holds. From current studies, persons with schizophrenia performed significantly worse compared to controls. The common areas of weaknesses for persons with schizophrenia included understanding, identifying, and managing emotions. Having low emotional intelligence scores was significantly correlated with increased difficulties in community functioning of an individual. The suggestion with this research is that emotional intelligence competencies can be used to help improve the life quality of individuals with various psychological conditions. Emotional intelligence can be used to further detector further improve existing mental illnesses, especially where personality disorders exist.

Furthermore, contemporary studies on emotional intelligence explore if emotional intelligence can be taught and if so can the information derived by an individual get retained over time. Some of the recent studies affirm that training groups on emotional intelligence will improve their emotional intelligence competencies. From the current studies finding, emotional intelligence competencies were still retained after six months. The implication of these studies and their findings is that emotional intelligence can be acquired and enhanced. Compared to intelligence quotient, emotional intelligence is highly coachable and also can be retained. Another implication of this study is that employers now have more freedom when hiring as they can still recruit a highly skilled individual and enroll the candidate for emotional intelligence training enabling the organization command a well-balanced workforce in terms of intelligence quotient and emotional intelligence competencies.

Lastly, new research on emotional intelligence focuses on the relationship between emotional intelligence and job performance. The connection between emotional intelligence and productivity was explored concentrating on the intersection between self-and other-focused emotional intelligence dimensions. Several studies affirm that emotion appraisal plays a significant role in subjective and objective job performance. As suggested above, emotional intelligence can help the question of why there is a gap in hiring a highly skilled candidate that has difficulties delivering perhaps due to challenges with working with others, communicating how he feels, and being tolerant. Most organizations deal with the public directly where how the organization communicates and handles a client counts more in some cases compared to the efficacy of the solution given.

Finally, current studies explore the possibility of emotional intelligence overlapping with personality and cognitive traits. Emotional intelligence tends to co-vary with cognitive abilities as well with personality traits. One of the other critical areas in human resource management is correct personality typing. Emotional intelligence can help increase correct personality typing compared to using only personality typing tests. Unlike personality tests, emotional intelligence measures actively profile the personality of a candidate. Emotional intelligence tests can infuse both ability and trait models of testing which can help correlate with the personality of an individual. There is a need in the future to investigate if emotional intelligence score correlates with cognitive and personality traits. For emphasis, the ability model of emotional intelligence enables evaluation of cognitive traits of an individual while the trait model aligns more with the personality of an individual.

Exercise

a. Assume that you are part of the board seeking to hire a candidate to replace the former network engineer at your Information Technology consultancy company. For this position, skills are highly critical as the successful candidate must actually perform the technical competencies specified. At the same time, the successful candidate has to work with others and train them on the organizational systems. It is apparent that you will require an individual that has significant mental abilities as well as emotional intelligence. After careful elimination, you have Richard, a highly skilled network engineer but appears to be emotionally unstable when asked questions that seem basic or offensive. On the other hand, you have Mike who has average skills and appears an average learner but has a great personality. As the final person, briefly describe how you would navigate this situation by prioritizing the company needs. Remember the needs of the company include getting a competent individual that must also work with others with ease.

Emotional intelligence framework

The emotional intelligence framework constitutes of three models that are the trait model, the ability model, and the mixed model. All these model focus on the application of knowledge and power to impact your emotional intelligence even though they differ significantly.

Starting with the ability model, it is an emotional intelligence framework that concerns perceiving emotions by understanding nonverbal signs such as the facial expressions of other people. The emotional intelligence framework also includes reasoning with emotions as emotional intelligence enhances thinking including a cognitive activity. Understanding emotions imply that one is interpreting the emotions of others around you and getting to acknowledge that people express emotions of anger when essentially they might not be angry at you but the situation. With respect to the ability framework, a person learns to manage emotions and react appropriately and consistently. For this reason, the ability framework uses self-awareness, self-regulation, motivation, empathy and social skills.

Secondly, there is a mixed framework that integrates different kinds of emotional intelligence qualities. Through this framework, we combine knowledge and understanding that concerns emotion triggers. Another aspect of the mixed approach is that it also covers skills such as empathy. Mixed approach framework concerns competencies such as the ability to detect facial expressions. There are also other components of the mixed model that include traits such as being optimistic and attitudes such as service orientation. Where possible, this model can also include other qualities such as being inspirational. It is challenging to assess all the aspects of emotional intelligence with one instrument and this call for the need to mix a variety of tools within one mega tool and then create an emotional quotient score.

Equally important when evaluating the mixed framework is how to process the proportion of each emotional intelligence basic tool that should be included. For example, do you use more items from the ability framework or from the trait framework? Another concern is how these combinations will impact the final outcome as each input data vary even though it is leading to the same objective. The proponents of this framework argue that it enables one to leverage on the strengths of each model and reduce the limitations of each individual model.

Additionally, there is the trait framework which largely constitutes self-reportage tools. Critics of this emotional intelligence framework think that self-perception is unreliable enough lest the tool is being used for personal reflection. It might be difficult to ascertain well how you perform at discerning your emotions and handle them as a type of thinking that gets clouded when having emotional meltdowns if your emotional intelligence is great. The major role of trait tools is that they will help you recognize how you view others and interact with them from an emotionally intelligent perspective. The focus on self-reportage is qualified because individuals are likely to relapse to inborn traits and self-reportage effectively brings this out.

Individuals that work in the domain of human behavior experience challenges about the believability of self-report concerning mental states. Usually, the issue of subjective experiences tends to dominate much of self-reportage that invites the question of bias. Individual bias impacts how he or she views others. Emotionally intelligence is a collection of competencies and skills that improve the performance of an individual at the workplace. In this manner, emotional intelligence should be handled as an interlinking of behavior motivated by social and emotional competencies that impact performance and behavior.

Correspondingly, emotional intelligence frameworks enable us to differentiate between emotions and emotional intelligence. Emotions can be considered as an inherent state of the mind that builds from the current environment, history, and contexts. The source of emotions includes circumstances, environment, and knowledge including relationships and moods. An individual's emotions are impacted by his or her feelings and experiences. Emotional intelligence is the skill, ability, and awareness to acknowledge, comprehend, and no particular feelings, emotions, and moods including applying them in a positive way. Learning how to manage feelings and emotions and apply that information to act and behave as well as making decisions, self-management, addressing your problems and leading others.

When evaluating the framework of emotional intelligence it is important to acknowledge that whereas the concept of emotional intelligence may seem a straightforward undertaking, it is not. The ability framework is treated as new intelligence and is limited to the standard criteria for all new intelligence. The ability framework scores emotional perception through taking into account the facial expression, voices, body language and pictures among others. Through emotional perception, you can recognize the emotions of others. Perceiving emotions is assumed to be a fundamental concept of emotional intelligence since it is important to complete any of the other requisite processes used in the ability framework.

Exercise
  a. Choose any aspect of the emotional intelligence framework and critique it

High and low emotional intelligence

The best way to differentiate high and low emotional intelligence is to present the attributes of each. A person with high emotional intelligence will express his or her feelings clearly and directly with three-word sentences such as "I feel like..." With high emotional intelligence, a person will not mask thoughts as feelings. When you have high emotional intelligence, you will not be afraid to manifest your feelings. Most importantly is that a person with high emotional intelligence will not be dominated by negative emotions. For instance, you will not be dominated by negative emotions such as guilt, shame, worry, obligation, powerlessness or embarrassment.

Additionally, an individual with high emotional intelligence reads nonverbal communication with ease. With high emotional intelligence, you will guide your feelings to precipitate healthy choices and reality. Persons that can balance feelings with logic, reason, and reality have high emotional intelligence. With high emotional intelligence, you will cat out of desire as opposed to acting due to force, duty, or obligation. With high emotional intelligence, you will be independent, morally autonomous and self-reliant. A person who is intrinsically motivated has high emotional intelligence. If an individual that is not motivated by wealth, power, fame, status or approval has attributes of emotional intelligence.

Furthermore, if you have high emotional intelligence then you are emotionally resilient. The other attributes of high emotional intelligence include feeling optimistic but also realistic and can allow certain levels of pessimism. With high emotional intelligence, an individual will not internalize failure. The competence of being interested in other people's feelings and being comfortable talking about feelings is considered part of high emotional intelligence. If a person is not immobilized by worry then the person is likely to have high emotional intelligence. The ability to identify multiple concurrent feelings helps build high emotional intelligence.

On the other hand, attributes of low emotional intelligence include not taking accountability for your feelings by blaming other people or the context. If one cannot explain how and why they are feeling then it is a sign of low emotional intelligence. A person with low emotional intelligence attempts to analyze you when you manifest your feelings. Such people start sentences with "I think you..." The messages of a person with low emotional intelligence tend to start with I think you should..." Individuals with low emotional intelligence will lay guilt trips on someone else. Another trait of low emotional intelligence is the tendency to withhold information about how one feels which emotional dishonesty is. If one has low emotional intelligence then he or she will minimize or exaggerate feelings.

Correspondingly, persons with low emotional intelligence will allow things to simmer until they blow up including reacting strongly to things that are relatively minor. Lacking integrity and a sense of conscience is a sign of low emotional intelligence. If one holds grudges and is unforgiving then the individual is showing attributes of low emotional intelligence. Expectedly, a person with low emotional intelligence is uncomfortable to be around. Such individuals act their emotions rather than expressing them out. When one is insensitive to how others feel including playing games by being evasive then it is a telling sign of low emotional intelligence. By having low emotional intelligence your compassion and empathy will be significantly low.

Similarly, low emotional intelligence can manifest as rigidity where the person is inflexible and needs rules and structure to feel assured. When one is not emotionally present and gives little opportunity to emotional intimacy then the person is exhibiting low emotional intelligence. An individual with low emotional intelligence will not take into account the feelings of others before acting. Another illustration of low emotional intelligence concerns an individual that is insecure and defensive and has difficulties to acknowledge mistakes as well as express remorse sincerely. Most individuals with low emotional intelligence cite the lack of other options to the way they reacted and behaved.

Equally important is that a low emotional intelligence individual will show a biased and stereotyped view of everything with persistent negative emotions. Such people might be excessively pessimistic and may invalidate the joy of others. Sometimes, persons with low emotional intelligence may be overly optimistic to the extent of being unrealistic and invalidate legitimate fears of others. If a person feels disappointed, inadequate, bitter, victimized or resentful then the person is likely to be exhibiting low emotional intelligence. Another illustration of low emotional intelligence is when the individual fixates himself into certain paths against common sense or makes a turn at the first instance of turmoil. When an individual seeks substitute relationships with pets and plants including imaginary beings and avoids connections with people than the person may be having low emotional intelligence.

By the same measure, low emotional intelligence will manifest as being clingy to your beliefs due to feeling insecure and avoiding embracing new concepts and views. A person with low emotional intelligence will describe the details of an event and what they think about it but will avoid telling you how they feel about it. Poor listeners that interrupt or invalidate others might be suffering from low emotional intelligence. The other attributes of low emotional intelligence include missing the emotions being expressed, focusing on facts as opposed to feelings.

Exercise

a. For one to be regarded as having a low emotional intelligence or a high emotional intelligence then the attributes suggested above have to be consistent and not just spontaneous attributes. Using the suggested attributed, describe a classmate or former classmate whom you classify as likely to have the low emotional intelligence or high emotional intelligence.

b. Look for a quiet place and review your actions over the last one to two weeks. Take out a piece of paper or a word processor application and label yourself "Candidate X". Rate the emotional intelligence of Candidate X as either high or low. State the characteristics of the settled on the classification of either low or high emotional intelligence.

Why developing emotional intelligence is crucial

Building emotional intelligence is important as emotions impact cognitive processes. For instance, one is likely to avoid taking the risk if he or she is feeling anxious. The feeling of anxiety makes one perceive the current environment as uncertain and avoiding risk is welcome when an individual feels unsure. Using this knowledge of emotions, intelligent traders will acknowledge that they will be risk-averse when they feel unsettled while traders with lower emotional intelligent might not be conscious of this effect. The illustration above suggests that high emotional intelligence may increase life success chances compared to low emotional intelligence. In overall, emotional intelligence influences cognitive processes and ultimately mediates or moderates our actions at the workplace and at home.

Notably, emotional intelligence can be used to harness emotions to inform cognitive activities and work out problems. The assertion here is that with requisite levels of emotional intelligence one can customize their cognitive activities to the situation at hand. Think of an individual that elicits thoughts of negative outcomes as a way of motivating performance at the workplace. Absolute control of emotions as well as generating corresponding emotions when they are not there to impact the cognitive processes will occur in persons with high emotional intelligence. On the other hand, with low emotional intelligence, it is difficult to trigger requisite emotions to influence the cognitive processes to enhance actual delivery at the workplace or any other context.

At a personal level still, emotional intelligence will enable you to understand your emotions. Through understanding your emotions you will get the power to handle the emotions. By having adequate attention to your thoughts and feelings it will become easier to manage your emotions. Handling your emotions frees you from volatile emotional reaction situations. An emotional outburst usurps most of your mental energy as well as physical energy. Through emotional intelligence, you will learn to slow down reaction to events and emotions and begin to discriminate your reactions to each situation. All of these developments will boost your self-confidence and assertiveness in life when you learn to handle your emotions.

Expectedly, emotional intelligence will make you understand yourself by discovering the specific areas that you need to improve. You can only work on your weakness if you understand the areas you are having difficulties at first. Fortunately, emotional intelligence includes self-awareness which is the process through which one comprehends herself. The competence that allows you to acknowledge emotions that you perceive is part of emotional awareness competencies. An example is where a student self-evaluates and realizes that he is too unease when receiving any form of negative feedback such as being reprimanded or being rejected by the opposite sex.

Another importance of developing emotional intelligence is that it enables an individual to understand emotion language. The ability to correctly acknowledge relations between emotions and words and place verbal labels to the individual and others' emotions is integral of emotional intelligence. There are individuals gifted with the ability to use the correct vocabulary that matches the emotional needs of the context. Such people realize when they are embarrassed and are likely to express how they feel using a requisite term. Even though it seems as another discussion on effective communication, the ability to understand emotion language goes beyond the standard demands of effective communication. In this case, the communicator deliberates seeks to understand the emotion the words used will elicit and also freely expresses his or her feelings during delivery.

Perhaps the best illustration of emotional intelligence can be found when the late former United Nations Secretary-General Koffi Annan lead negotiation in Kenya when the country was experiencing post-election violence that almost turned into national civil war. Each of the antagonizing sides was emotionally charged and repeatedly attempted to derail the mindset of the late Koffi Annan. As a lead mediator, the late Koffi Annan managed to maintain calmness and sought to listen to each side by acknowledging their frustrations and other emotions while also allowing his emotions to manifest but under control. Emotional intelligence increases your ability to remain calm in an emotionally charged environment and this gives you more control and value.

By learning emotional intelligence one learns to employ requisite emotion regulation strategies. Earlier on we suggested that understanding your emotions are important but that might not help if you cannot deploy ways to manage the identified emotions. Fortunately, emotional intelligence covers strategies for handling particular emotions. Think of when you realize that you become emotional when receiving negative feedback in public. Now that you know your weakness, you will need a matching strategy to handle that emotion. Through emotional intelligence competencies such self-awareness, social skills, and anger management you will learn how to safely express the negative emotion.

Exercise
  a. In your own understanding, state three ways that makes developing emotional intelligence important at a personal level.

Self and relationship management

For emphasis, you can only relate well with others if you can relate well with your inner self. Good relationship management should begin with inner self and extend to the external space. Focusing on the self, emotional intelligence influences your actions and thoughts as it is self-reinforcing. Think of when you are angry and bang the table, after some time you think again about the unsolved situation that made you bang the table and might walk away in protest or feel emotionally and physically drained. All these feelings and actions reinforce each other extending the cycle. It takes emotional intelligence to break or manage this cycle.

When one has requisite levels of emotional intelligence, he or she will improve the manner in which you handle or identify the emotions including the matching reaction to feelings of others. When one becomes emotionally stable, he or she starts to grow and gain an extensive comprehension of which we are and this enables us to communicate better than others. It is only possible to sustain a stronger relationship with others when we have requisite emotional intelligence levels. For instance, practice capturing how you feel and try to link to how you express it. It is important that you let your emotions manifest as opposed to locking up the emotions.

With good individual emotional intelligence, you will start working on your social skills which improve relationship management. When interacting with people you have to become aware of your emotions and reactions as well as those of others. The process of attending to your emotional need as well as acknowledging the emotional needs of others is a critical part of relationship management. Each person in a group wants to be where he or she is accommodated and respected. All of these needs are highly perceptual meaning body language, diction and tone of communication, as well as actions, impact the relationship in a big way. Think of narrating to your supervisor that you were unwell and the supervisor is busy typing listening to music.

Another important aspect of self and relationship management is how to handle assertiveness. Being assertive does not imply being domineering but simply making your position known and seeking others to acknowledge and respect it. Assertiveness in a relationship can be a source of friction when either of the parties does not acknowledge the concept of assertiveness. Think of an individual trying to assert his opinion and the other person misconstruing that to mean that the former's opinion has to prevail at whatever cost. Fortunately, emotional intelligence enables one to perceive the reactions of the other person and take into consideration when asserting his or her views.

Similarly, being aware of how you behave constitutes part of self and relationship management. If you are not aware of your actions then you are not aware of how they impact others. In a relationship framework, one must always think of how your individual actions will affect others. Through emotional intelligence, learn to notice and note your behavior. With practice, try to note the particular feeling and the matching reaction that you express. The intent of this element in operationalizing emotional intelligence is to become aware of your emotions and how you react to them to have better management of them. Your individual emotions will impact the relationship with others.

Another issue that may affect self and relationships concerns recognizing and discarding ingrained stereotypes and bias. If we become honest, we have ingrained stereotypes and biases against certain religions, races, sexes and places and this subtly manifest in our emotional reaction and communication including behaviors. It is important that one learns to interrogate his or her opinions as a form of self-evaluation to notice any form of stereotype and bias. An emotional reaction that exhibits elements of bias or stereotypes will significantly strain your relationship with others as your weaknesses with respect to emotional intelligence will be perceived as intentional even when they are not.

Last but not least, become accountable to one and to others. Taking responsibility for your emotions, reactions and corresponding actions are critical in building honest and sustainable relationships. One must learn to be accountable to self before expressing accountability in a group setting. Think of a colleague that spoke rudely to a customer but the offending colleague does not want to account for the negative feedback that the customer gave and now the whole sales team that day is left to shoulder the blame of an individual. Without a doubt, all this will strain the relationship in that sales team.

Exercise

a. The author makes an assertion that a good relationship can only happen when each individual works on their emotional intelligence. Do you agree or disagree with this assertion? Why or Why not?

b. Give your own experience of how the self and relationship management worked or did not work.

Emotional intelligence in the workplace

Predictably, emotional intelligence counts at the workplace in several ways. One of the ways that emotional intelligence impacts businesses are that emotional intelligence can spur improved business decisions. Making decisions involves a series of eliciting information and reasoning it out as a group. Most business decisions are reached through meetings and such meetings require each participant to remain cognizant of their emotions and those of others including their reactions. With an environment that appreciates and respects each member, all members are likely to actively and honestly participate in brainstorming sessions leading to rich, multiple views of the issues at hand. In this manner, emotional intelligence has been applied to making the meeting respectful and accommodating to everyone. The other way that emotional intelligence increases the quality of business decisions is by thinking of how the recipients of the decisions will react and behave and adjusting the final decision accordingly.

Additionally, employees with threshold emotional intelligence are likely to act civil and dignified. Employees that have at least average levels of emotional intelligence are likely to be accommodative, considerate and respectful when interacting with others and the public. Emotional intelligence requires one to determine their weaknesses and act on them in the context of emotional intelligence. When an employee recognizes their ingrained biases and seeks ways to eliminate this bias, they are likely to appear open-minded and this will make it easier to interact with diverse groups. By thinking about how others feel or will feel will enable an employee to adjust the diction and reaction to be sensitive to others. The modern workplace is a diverse environment having different ethnicities, genders, religious affiliations, and sexual orientations which calls for an accommodative workforce.

Equally important is that employees with high emotional intelligence are likely to resolve conflicts with more success compared to those that do not. Conflicts are unavoidable because of the unique nature of human behavior and the human mind. A diverse work environment increases the risk of conflicts. When conflicts occur, employees with emotional intelligence are likely to resolve their conflicts with easy as the competencies of emotional intelligence requires one to think about how others feel. Conflict resolution competencies are also among derived competencies of emotional intelligence. The practice of learning to let go of bias and consider how others feel can significantly deescalate a simmering tension in an organization and all these are applications of competencies of emotional intelligence.

Furthermore, leaders that have high emotional intelligence are likely to manifest greater empathy. Another aspect of emotional intelligence usefulness at workplace concerns the leaders of teams. The actions and reactions of leaders will impact team productivity and eventually the overall productivity of the organization. A leader that has high emotional intelligence is likely to be perceived as empathetic and this is likely to enhance the appeal of the leader to the team. The other importance of having a leader with high emotional intelligence is that the leader is likely to read the impact of new guidelines and changes even before they are implemented and enhance their success.

Correspondingly, employees with high emotional intelligence are likely to reflect, listen, and respond to constructive criticism. For emphasis, employees that exhibit high emotional intelligence are likely to engage in self-reflection, listen keenly, and respond to useful criticism. Self-reflection is critical for continuous employee improvement and in some professionals is directly related to quality such as in the healthcare field. Most individuals have challenges responding to criticism even where such criticism is constructive. Fortunately, emotional intelligence prepares each person to seek and welcome feedback and learn from it. Against this backdrop, employees that exhibit high levels of emotional intelligence are likely to improve by embracing and learning from constructive criticism. In overall, the productivity of the workforce of the organization will improve when its workers exhibit high levels of emotional intelligence.

Some of the ways that employees can enhance their emotional intelligence are through becoming self-aware. An individual should take note of how they are feeling at the instance of the day. Ask yourself how the observed emotions impact your response. It is necessary that you determine your emotions and how they influence your routine activities. Make an assessment of your emotional weaknesses and strengths. For instance, anger is an emotion but how you express or manage it might be a weakness. Against this backdrop, negative emotions are not weaknesses but how one reacts and manages negative emotions such as banging on the table when angry is an emotional weakness. Allowing anger to prolong its manifest on your mind is a weakness.

Exercise

a. Using two to three sentences give an overview of how emotional intelligence impacts workplaces.

b. Why do you think emotional intelligence is critical in a diverse workplace?

Emotional intelligence and relationships

When applied to relationships, emotional intelligence will enhance the value and experience of relationships. One of the ways that emotional intelligence impacts relationships are that it enables the individual to read the emotions of others. As insinuated earlier, healthy relationships flourish when we learn to acknowledge and respect the emotions of others. Recognizing the emotions of others makes them feel we care and that we are connected on so many levels. The competencies of acknowledging the emotions of others constitute emotional intelligence competencies that include self-awareness and emotional regulation among others. Think of being part of a group where the feeling of each member is acknowledged and respected. The members of that team will feel connected and appreciated and will be free with each other.

Secondly, individuals that are emotionally intelligent will listen to understand and manage their individual emotions. Understanding yourself and the other person is integral to emotional intelligence competencies. Learning to listen empathetically allows you to capture the tone and mood of the communication which makes you understand the message deeper. Understanding the message being communicated is vital to recognize how the other person feels and respecting the feeling rather than judging it. However, during active listening, there is a possibility of your emotions getting triggered and this requires one to effectively manage these emotions. Think of listening to a colleague that is complaining about the supervisor not knowing that the supervisor was your classmate. In this illustration, while listening actively, your individual emotions are likely to be activated and it is vital that you manage the emotions.

Thirdly, emotional intelligence will enable you to understand that your thoughts trigger emotions and managing the thoughts helps regulate the emotions. Most individuals overlook the power of their thoughts in triggering emotions and subsequent emotional reactions. Our human emotions are a function of our thoughts and this realization implies that we can control our emotions by managing our thoughts. For every one of us, it is easier to control thoughts before they become emotions. Emotions require a full release to restore balance but with thoughts, we can safely interrupt them without significant harm to the balance of the mind. In this aspect, one must understand his or her thoughts and activate strategies of managing such thoughts before they graduate into emotions. For instance, when you entertain the thought that you are worthless and not valued at the workplace, you are likely to become agitated and withdrawn.

Fourthly, an emotionally intelligent person will acknowledge that there is a link between one's actions and emotional reactions of other people. How we react emotionally influences our actions. The presence of this relationship should motivate us to manage our emotions to improve the way we behave as this impacts others. Using the same example of feeling agitated, you are likely to walk continuously and appear unsettled and are likely not to listen to other people trying to speak to you. Expectedly, such people might either feel that you are ignoring them or that they might notice that you are agitated. Your reaction may continue affecting them as they might avoid bringing a report at your desk or they might informally meet to decipher what is bothering you. The conclusion of this argument is that our individual emotions and actions may have a propagating negative or positive effect on those we relate with.

Fifthly, determine what calms you down and utilize it. When it comes to applying emotional intelligence in a relationship, it is important to discover what works for you and utilize it as often you can. Using the example of agitation, for some people walking helps them drop the anger. For some people when agitated and at home they prefer dancing. The common attribute of what helps you defuse an emotion is that you have to engage in another activity that distracts you from the thoughts and converts the emotional energy into physical energy. In most cases, seeking to convert emotional energy into physical energy will work but unfortunately when this conversation leads to harm then the approach should be unethical at best and criminal at worst.

Sixthly, pay attention to social awareness to enable you to control your thoughts in the long-term. Since we realized that thoughts trigger emotions, the core focus when managing emotions should be on your thoughts. A keen exploration of the issue makes us conclude that the environment influences our thoughts through past experiences, environmental triggers, and context of the situation. For this reason, social awareness is critical in managing thoughts and eventually managing emotions leading to healthy relationships. If you possess social awareness then you have significant control of your thoughts and consequently your emotions.

Exercise

a. The writer makes an interesting assertion that one of the effective ways of managing emotional energy is to convert into physical energy. For instance, when feeling disappointed you can jog around the track to deviate your mind from the negative thought and corresponding emotion. Do you agree? If not, why?

Chapter 2: The Application of Emotional Intelligence

Handling Impulses

A sudden thought or emotion that is overwhelming is known as an impulse. With respect to emotional intelligence, an impulse is an irresistible emotion or urge. Regulating an impulse will involve purposely seeking to increase or lower the intensity of emotion as well as committing not to act on a desire. The requisite skills for managing an impulse include decision and control of where you direct attention to. Recall that our emotions originate from our thoughts and the implication of this revelation is that learning to control our thoughts will lead to improved management of the emotions. You can direct your attention to or away from certain thoughts as a way of handling impulses. Against this backdrop, learning to make a decision and managing where you direct your attention to will lead to improved management of impulses.

Additionally, one should learn to stop the temptation to act on a desire. For this measure, you should develop emotional awareness as well as social awareness. One of the ways to develop emotional awareness is to create a journal of specific emotions and how you reacted to it. With a journal of the frequent emotions and how they manifest, one can develop an intervention that seeks to slow down or stop the trigger factors that cause that emotion. If you feel irritated on certain days and you manage to determine the underlying causes, then it is advisable to manage those factors as opposed to managing the subsequent reaction. The desire is to let out your entire anger manifest while the suggested intervention is to discourage your mind enjoying full control of the emotion. Expectedly, this measure is learned through practice over a considerable period of time.

Furthermore, it is necessary to think about things that calm you when you feel highly emotional. When you feel exhilarated or irritated, it is suggested that deviate your mind to thinks that calm your mind. When activating this intervention, you may have to temporarily depart from the current moment to enable you to take your mind to past experiences that elicit calmness. For instance, you may think of the moment when your favorite team won and you jumped up in celebration and admiration of their resilience when facing a disappointing situation. On the other hand, you might divert your mind to a past experience where you were excited and went on a spending spree leading to difficulties sustaining your routine expenses when feeling exhilarated on receiving a salary increment. The emphasis here is that learn to divert your mind to things that calm when highly excited or irritated.

Correspondingly, it is important to develop adaptability by demonstrating flexibility when facing changing situations is critical in fighting off impulses. Difficulties with managing impulses suggest that the individual has challenges with allowing the mind and body to adjust. Expectedly, allowing impulses is appealing as it is a way of letting your mind and body desires to triumph and cost least mental energy initially. Fortunately, by learning to be adaptable by embracing flexibility in thoughts and actions will increase your competencies of handling impulses. For instance, instead of always of expressing your anger due to feeling disappointed you can accept that sometimes one must be ridiculed. Once you add some room of alternative outcome and reaction to a specific emotion then you can safely exit the emotional meltdown through selecting the least adverse action.

It is also necessary that you develop a set of values that helps checks your desires. It is important that one develops a set of values and principles that guides the individual in any situation. In essence, when one has a set of values, he or she is simply trying to train the mind to learn to act in a certain manner that might be against the impulses. For instance, if one of your values is to remain calm in any situation then you are explicitly training your mind to accept disappointments and process the anger in a civil manner. Against this backdrop, developing a set of values helps demarcate the limit of your impulses and sets the path to developing emotional awareness and self-regulation.

Exercise

a. List any three impulses that you face or have faced.

b. Suggest ways that you can increase management of these impulses through emotional intelligence competencies.

c. In earlier segments of the book, the author encouraged the expression of emotions by arguing that emotions are a form of energy and it must be dissipated to help restore the emotional balance of the mind. However, under this segment, the author is suggesting that one should control impulses. The main reason for this argument is that impulses are unique aspects of emotions as you temporarily lose any form of control of the emotion. Do you agree with this assertion? Why or why not?

Handling difficulties and setbacks

Difficulty situations will always exist because at one point we are taking risks as well as the fact that there are external factors beyond our control. One of the effective ways of handling setbacks is to select the situation by avoiding circumstances that activate adverse emotions. For instance, if you feel irritated when a deadline is fast approaching then it is suggested that you start planning and working earlier by splitting the work into modules. You can go further and inform your colleagues that short deadlines may make you react adversely. Where possible, change the environment to get away from triggers especially where the triggers are not human entities. If you are under pressure to complete a task then a noisy environment may aggravate your emotional reaction to the situation. Changing the environment or seeking to eliminate noise, in this case, might improve your handling of the approaching deadline.

Secondly, learn to adapt to the situation. The main qualification for vouching for modifying the situation stems from the realization that we cannot always control every situation. For situations we cannot control, learning to adjust to the situation is helpful to avoid a negative emotional reaction. For instance, if you are fired from work, it is important that you do not get stuck fighting the disappointment forever. It would help if you adjust your mind and lifestyle to the new status of an unemployed person. With the adjustment, it becomes much easier to start rebuilding your ambitions and your life. Individuals that are unable to learn and unlearn might have difficulties adjusting to situations which increases the likelihood of adverse emotional reactions. However, they are some situations where even individuals with high emotional intelligence might have difficulties adjusting such as grieving or divorce.

It is also important that you learn to redirect your focus. It is human to want to excel and be counted among the influential people. For this reason, our minds tend to focus on our ambitions or what we consider as the ideal life. The continued burden on the mind to process only positive news and desires increases the uneasiness and inability to acknowledge and process negative feedback in routine interactions. For example, you competed in a sports activity and your team was bundled out. All team members feel disappointed but you are also angry at one of the team members who reported for training late and you feel he could have performed better. Each time you let your mind wander on the possibilities that your ream would be having been it not for that one member your negative emotions aggravates.

Related to the previous strategies in handling setbacks is changing your thoughts. As indicated earlier on, thoughts impact emotions and eventually the emotional reaction. While it appears easy, changing thoughts might be a challenge on its account. Changing thoughts requires letting the mind let go of something it is trying to resolve. Fortunately, using cognitive reappraisal you can replace adverse thoughts with constructive thoughts. Additionally, by learning to relax the mind you increase your abilities to navigate difficult situations. There is a possibility that sticking to negative thoughts might be related to self-esteem issues but everyone tends to grapple with negative thoughts as a way of resolving a challenging situation. With good practice, you will learn to drop negative thoughts by replacing them with positive ones.

Sometimes everything might fail and in that case, emotional regulation is the best measure. In this strategy, an individual focuses on managing the emotions that are manifesting. For instance, you are unable to prevent an episode of anger so you focus on handling the simmering anger by walking away, going to the washroom, playing music or informing the other person to take a break because you are irritated.

Some people manage anger by sitting down, changing facial expressions or walking down the stairs than up. For emphasis, emotional regulation can be for both positive and negative emotions. Being highly excited can make it difficult to continue with a conversation of discussion and you should think of how winners of music awards or lotteries behave. Think of someone that cannot stop laughing when everyone else is sad.

Exercise

a. Collins works in one of the leading exporters of spectacles. Due to the nature of the products the company has a strict work routine as well as a strict work routine. Collins is the supervisor of a team of 14 people. When the team fails to process orders on time and the client is issuing threats of canceling the order, Collins become anxious, agitated and sometimes almost abusive. From this narrative identify the challenging situation? Assuming that delays with processing cannot be completely eliminated, how can Collins improve his reaction to setbacks? How can employees working under Collins improve how they handle the challenging situation which is a boss that might not understand they are not to blame?

Handling stress and anxiety

First, identify the origin of the stress. Like with any problem, you can only develop an effective solution when you understand the trigger of your stress. Even though it appears a straightforward endeavor it is not. Some of the major stressors include moving, changing jobs, going through a divorce or increased workload either at home or workplace. One of the areas that contribute to stress and that we overlook is our individual thoughts, behaviors, and feelings that increase routine stress levels. For instance, it might not the job that is stressing but fear of not delivering on that job. An effective strategy to determine the source of anxiety is to keep a journal of the emotion and the corresponding reaction. From the personal journal of your emotions, you will get an opportunity to evaluate your anxiety and the triggers.

Secondly, accept that you have stress and anxiety. The second major step in managing stress is to acknowledge that you have it. Most individuals with stress and anxiety rarely accept that they have the condition until late. Part of this reluctance of accepting stress and anxiety is because it is portrayed as a form of mental weakness and an inability to cope with demanding situations. All these stereotypes package one as not employable because all workplaces have demanding situations. However, stress and anxiety is not a weakness but an acknowledgment of your body that it has reached the known limit which is specific to each individual. For this reason, one should learn to determine their individual stress levels as they differ per individual and they are not a weakness but an affirmation that your body feedback loop is working.

Thirdly, recognize and accept your role in creating stress and anxiety. Another flaw in handling stress and anxiety is when we blame situations and people other than ourselves. The truth is that we participate in precipitating stress and anxiety. For instance, if you fail to plan for work during peak season at your workplaces chances are that you are going to face heightened workload within a short period of time. If you fail to adequately participate in social moments then chances are that you are likely to bottle up emotions that might precipitate anxiety. When you acknowledge the role you play in creating the stress and anxiety then you will commit to enhancing that role to precipitate positive outcomes with respect to anxiety management.

Fourthly, even with these measures, it is still important that you maintain a stress journal. The purpose of the stress journal is to help you identify routine triggers of stress in your life and the manner that you intervene. You are likely to realize that in most cases, you rarely intervene to these stressors or you consistently apply ineffective interventions. The other purpose of a stress journal is to help you develop a long-term effective intervention plan after determining the nature of the triggers of stress and how you normally react to the stress. While this suggestion appears easy to implement, most people do not always feel motivated to write down one of their challenging moments but with multiple attempts, you will manage to keep a stress journal.

Additionally, one should avoid unnecessary stress and anxiety. After identifying the sources of stress in your life, you are likely to acknowledge that not all of these sources are necessary. For instance, being overly worried about your productivity at the workplace is not necessary if you plan and understand your job tasks well. If you learn to let go of thoughts of disappointment and accept that we all cannot attain the same level at the same time, you will start focusing on the positive aspects of your life. If you define your limits and assert them then some of the pressures that you invite can be eased. Indeed, stress is not completely avoidable but not all stress is necessary. For instance, you can choose to avoid people that wear you out emotionally.

Last but not least, manage your environment. The environment contributes a significant part of your stress and anxiety but it can be managed to a limited extent. For example, if evening news makes you edgy you can turn off the TV. If traffic makes you agitated, you can leave the house earlier than you normally do or use a different route. Another way of managing the environmental factors that trigger stress is to list to-do-list and how you will accomplish the action and what happens when you cannot. In essence, you are giving an action plan as well as a contingency plan.

Exercise

a. Sometimes it is difficult to prevent a stressful situation. In this case, one should consider altering the situation to increase chances of defusing anxiety or stress. From your past experience, list any two moments where you felt stress that you could not navigate through and how you finally overcame it.

In the workplace

Indeed emotional intelligence is critical at the workplace in multiple ways. One of the ways that emotional intelligence is useful in the workplace is to help each one of us understand our emotions and how they affect others. There are a number of people that do not recognize their emotions and this makes difficult for them to manage them as well as acknowledge how their reactions impact others. Fortunately, emotional intelligence can help an employee acknowledge their emotions and seek to exercise self-regulation to avoid making their emotions a liability. Workplaces are increasingly becoming diverse and it is important that we acknowledge our emotions and how manifesting they will impact people of other ethnicities, gender, sexual orientation, and different faiths. For instance, if you are angry and express that anger when speaking to a minority group they might interpret your emotional reaction as belittling them or their efforts.

Additionally, emotional intelligence enables employees to build social skills. Employees mostly work with others and the public. Emotional intelligence is a fundamental of social intelligence. Employees use emotional intelligence to visualize how the other person is feeling and adjust the communication to be considerate yet effective. In the absence of emotional intelligence, an employee would not care much about how the other person is feeling and effectively lack social skills. It can be argued that possessing high emotional intelligence predisposes one to high social skills that are admired at workplaces. Think of a high qualified engineer that is regarded as temperamental and most workers avoid engaging him on challenging issues. Workplaces are modularized and each category of employees must effortlessly interact with others in the organization.

Furthermore, emotional intelligence can help employees understand their actions to customers and the public at large. When employees understand how the public will feel then they will act in a manner that is considerate. Think of an employee that understands that developing an ineffective solution will irritate the customer; such an employee is likely to diligently work to offer an effective solution to customers. At the forefront employees that have high emotional intelligence are likely to relate well with customers by listening empathetically and speaking with consideration. From these illustrations, emotional intelligence helps humanize employee actions which give the organization a human face. Think of the businesses that handle you with respect and appear keen to listen and act on your feedback.

Another importance of emotional intelligence is that it can help improve routine communication. Employees are forever entangled in grapevine communication at workplaces. It is during this form of communication that some employees feel unease or offended by their colleagues. The uneasiness can easily spiral into entrenched dislikes of each other and affect productivity. However, with emotional intelligence, all employees learn to read the feelings of others and even predict how their colleague will react to certain communication. Using emotional intelligence, the communicator will adjust or stop the communication if it makes others unease. Think of one of your colleagues making fun of Muslims not knowing that your in-laws are Muslims and wondering why you seem disinterested in the joke.

For leaders, emotional intelligence can help leaders cultivate their empathy attribute. A leader with high levels of emotional intelligence is likely to be perceived as a listening and approachable leader. An empathetic leader listens to the emotions of the audience and pays attention to the emotional value of the communication. Simply put, a leader with high emotional intelligence is a listening leader and members of the team are likely to feel valued in such a setup. Now think of a leader who cares not about how others feel when communicating. The members of such a team are likely to feel undervalued and demotivated. The advantage of having a motivated team is that there is less need for supervision and employee turnover is low.

Equally important is that emotional intelligence is critical to solving conflicts. As indicated earlier on, conflicts are unavoidable at workplaces. With increased diversity at the workplace, the frequency of conflicts will only increase. Fortunately, with emotional intelligence that explores self-regulation, emotional awareness and social skills the communication of each employee to the other is likely to be considerate. Each time employees disagree, they are likely to see the justification for the disagreement as opposed to precipitating a crisis. Manifesting emotions in a diverse workplace can aggravate conflicts as the communication and actions may be misinterpreted as entrenching discrimination. Emotional intelligence is a critical means to defuse tensions before they graduate into conflicts.

Exercise

a. Emotional intelligence is widely applied at the workplace, to enhance interactions among employees, to improve the relationship of the organization and clients, to increase the effectiveness of a leader, and to help defuse conflicts. Pick one of these areas and describe how emotional intelligence can help improve workplace environment or organization's human face.

Coping with trauma

Trauma arises when one goes through a disturbing event and feels overwhelmed. For instance, near-death injury and torture can trigger trauma. Trauma should be acknowledged and viewed as an acute stress event. Like any mental health issue, the first step to manage it is to accept that it is present. A number of affected people might not accept that they are suffering from trauma or the might not understand that they have trauma. The initial step to coping with trauma is to help the individual acknowledge that they are suffering from trauma. As suggested earlier, most people have a negative view of any mental health as it is seen as having a weakness. It is important to underscore that trauma is a way of the mind forcing you to seek closure from a disturbing experience to restore balance.

Secondly, note the triggers that worsen relapse of the intense fear that you experience. For instance being left alone, avoidance of loud noise and being startled by sudden movements. Just like stress and anxiety, trauma has triggers that we should identify. For instance, if you were shot at in a noisy environment then each time you hear or walk into a noisy environment your mind will work you through the past gruesome event. It is important to understand that your mind is trying to protect from harm by activating the extreme reaction you exhibited when your life your threat. In this manner, coping with trauma is a way of minimizing the gruesome memory to allow your mind to stop treating any minor disturbance as a potentially grave threat to your life.

Thirdly, note your reactions each time you relive the traumatic experience such as lack of sleep, guilt, withdrawing to oneself, and anger. With time you will notice that you react differently to each trigger of your trauma. For instance, you might physically lock up your environment each time you hear movements outside. Other people might inadvertently scream when a car suddenly breaks. Try to write down each trigger and your reaction. For instance, you might write "Movements outside-I hurriedly closed the door and kept quiet". Using the example above, the trigger for reliving trauma was movements outside and your reactions were closing the door. By maintaining a journal of triggers and how you reacted, you will have adequate information to help design an intervention to manage trauma.

Fourthly, design a plan to handle the emotional reactions. Before working on the underlying cause, it is important to handle the emotional manifestations as they can be a danger to oneself and others. It is important to design an intervention plan to manage the reaction due to triggers as some of the reaction can pose danger to yourself and others. Think of each time you hear a bang your instinct is to jump due to past gruesome experience with a lone gunman. A person with this reaction can harm himself if standing near a balcony or any other place where impulse movement can pose danger. An immediate intervention plan should focus on degrading the intensity of the reaction of a person suffering from trauma.

Fifthly, design an intervention to handle the underlying traumatic event. For a long-term solution, it is important to address the underlying cause. Start by letting the person drop the self-blame for predisposing himself or herself to the way of harm. It takes time for victims of trauma to drop self-blame. The temptation for self-blame by the victim is to enable them not embark on the journey of seeking justice that reminds them of the circumstances that led to the gruesome experience and aggravate the self-blame. Sometimes it might be necessary to visit or recreate the event to help the individual walk the mind through the situation several times to gain mental stamina. In other cases, it might require extracting the individual from the physical environment to eliminate physical reminders of the unfortunate incident.

Lastly, confront situations linked to traumatic events gradually but exhaustively. While it is important to address the underlying factors that led to trauma, it is also important to address other issues that relate to the unfortunate event. For instance, assume that Richard was assaulted by armed robbers in his house, one week after moving in a new neighborhood. After addressing the circumstances directly related to the unfortunate incident it is also important to tackle other issues that might have precipitated the incident including those that Richard has no control over. For instance, Richard highly social nature that includes inviting fresh acquaintances and posting about his house furnishings on social media. Care should be exercised when confronting situations that caused the traumatic events so as not to appear to be judging the event.

Exercise

a. Recall any movie that depicts a traumatic event of a lead character. How did the lead character react or cope with the situation?

b. Search the Internet and read about survivors of 9/11 terror attacks in the United States are coping with the trauma.

Coping with reactions

Coping with emotional reactions concerns how and when to manifest emotions we feel. First, become aware of your emotions. Before managing emotions, you need to understand and acknowledge the emotions by knowing why you are feeling that way. By understanding your emotions you will manage to understand why you react the way you do. For emphasis, most people assume they know or do not need to know their emotions. Without the knowledge that the emotion that you experiencing is anger, you will not appreciate why you shout, walk away or bang the table. In the absence of knowledge of the type of emotions manifesting you will struggle to handle the reaction. Keeping an emotional journal can help one comprehend the frequency and type of emotions manifesting and lead to better coping mechanisms.

Secondly, learn to safely express your emotions. Emotions are a form of energy and locking them up will not help. Learning to safely express your emotions is important. For instance, the author suggested that the best way to handle emotions is to convert the emotions into physical energy from emotional energy. In this manner, when your anger starts building, you can start dancing, wash your face continuously or take a walk. However, in reality, you will not always get an opportunity to convert emotional energy into physical energy and these calls for other ways to manage emotional reactions. One of the ways to attain coping to a reaction is to anticipate the emotion and define the reaction including the limit of that reaction.

Thirdly, seek feedback and improve. Like with any learning process, you need to seek feedback about your emotional intelligence and commit to learning. For instance, you can ask colleagues to rate your temper. When asking for feedback it is important not to view the information given as profiling you. The colleagues are simply giving you information based on the way you interact with them. If your colleagues say you are temperamental do not pin them down or justify your temper. The intent of getting feedback is to get the views of other people and look for ways to remedy the suggested shortcomings. Using the information solicited use emotional intelligence to work on your weak areas that include not feeling interested in the conversation of others.

Fourthly, develop multiple options and weigh on which one is beneficial. Most people do not realize that they have a choice when it comes to emotional reactions. For instance, you do not need to reply to every statement made against you. Sometimes you just need to acknowledge that your personality and your delivery are different though related. By criticizing your output does not necessarily mean that they are criticizing the whole you. When facing backlash for the work you did, you can choose to process the feedback as judging your delivery or personality. If you take this into account, you will realize that you do not need to react the way you do in most circumstances. Additionally, you can choose to substitute anger with a positive feeling.

Fifthly, learn to unlearn. One of the overlooked competencies is the ability to unlearn. Most people can learn but cannot unlearn. The ability to unlearn allows you to restructure thoughts, emotions, and reactions. High coping levels are likely to manifest in individuals that unlearn. Our emotional reactions are impulsive and it takes a mental effort to drop convenience of manifesting our feelings. Expectedly, shouting or crying when angry will make you feel at peace but it is not the most appropriate reactions when working with people. Coping with reactions should not be misconstrued to mean bottling up emotions but rather safely expressing emotions by being considerate to others. The intent of this strategy is to urge you to unlearn impulsive reaction to negative emotions such as screaming or banging the table.

Finally, account for your reactions. It is important you become for the reactions you show to your emotions. By being accountable to your reactions you will appreciate their value and burden and seek to maximize their good value and minimize their cost. An emotional reaction has value and cost. When you are angry and shout at others, the value of the reaction is that it quickly dissipates your anger and the cost of the reaction is that you appear volatile and other people will be uneasy being around you. Most people blame situations or other things rather than taking up responsibilities to the way they reacted.

Exercise

a. How do you handle disappointment when alone?

b. Similarly, how do you handle disappointment when with people?

Chapter 3: Recognizing Emotions

Common and negative emotions in the workplace

Envy

One of the common workplace emotions is envy and the emotion is allowed to manifest as each one of us admires to be accomplished. It is allowed for human beings to nurse and pursue ambitions routinely. However, when one becomes uneasy with the achievement of others to the point of being affected mentally and physically then the feeling is envy. Like any other mental condition, persons that are envious rarely accept that they have a negative emotion. Envy is likely to affect the workplace negatively. Even though a limited and occasional form of envy is welcome as a necessary trigger to improve and strive, if it becomes unmanaged it becomes an adverse emotion. Since workplaces appraise their employees, individual employees are likely to admire to accomplish more like their feted colleagues and this can breed feelings of envy.

Correspondingly, one of the ways of recognizing a feeling of envy is when you persistently feel that you deserved the reward bestowed on your colleagues. Even though workplace systems might not always play fair, in most cases they closely capture the natural setup of the organization and individual as well as group contributions. It is expected for some employees especially the lowly rated ones in terms of productivity or personality to feel unease with the ranking system at the organization. However, the feeling of resentment becomes envy when one persistently feels that he or she deserved the reward and not the current winners of the reward. If it becomes difficult to let go of this feeling for days to months then you are probably envious and this will negatively affect your delivery at the workplace.

Additionally, when one entertains the thoughts of working underhand to upset the candidate who appears accomplished at the workplace then envious feelings are manifesting. If unmanaged, envy can push an individual to scheme to degrade the performance of celebrated colleagues at the workplace. Think of a jealous employee that seeks to sabotage the work that was left unsaved by a colleague celebrated as a highly accomplished worker. In extreme circumstances, envy can lead to unwarranted disagreements and attempts to have the targeted accomplished colleague fired or face disciplinary action. Take the case of Janet who is envious of the achievements of Mark at the workplace and manages to find Mark's computer on and open. She then manages to use the log in the email of Mark to send pranks to several colleagues without the knowledge of Mark. In this case, the intention of Janet is to malign Mark because she is envious of him.

If each time you interact or work with certain colleagues, that are recognized at the workplace and you feel a sense of jealousy when you are likely envious of their achievement. Sometimes envy might appear as jealousy which means you feel heightened suspicion of your colleagues. Take the case of Janet who views everything Mark suggests with suspicion. In the mind of Janet, all suggestions of Mark are meant to make him flourish at the workplace and for this reason; she doubts and questions every suggestion of Mark. So far Mark has been restrained but he is starting to notice that Janet might have a general disliking of his personality. Like any other feeling, a limited and infrequent manifestation of envy is welcome but when it persists then it becomes a liability to the individual and the entire organization.

On the extreme scale, you might incessantly seek to make everyone aware of your contribution when working in a group which is a manifestation of envy.

Sometimes envy is expressed with incessant attempts to seek validation. When envy is unmanaged an individual might seek to broadcast his or her every contribution in each task to attract attention to their productivity value in the group and indeed the entire organization. The reason for such individuals broadcasting their contribution to the team is to explicitly nominate their self for rewards. In other words, unjustified completion at the workplace can be a form of envy. Such kind of envy might make the affected individual make unjustified communication in the form of reports and send them to the supervisor of teammates.

Lastly, an individual with envy might embark on unplanned career development including seeking more workload than necessary. Envy is related to uncontrolled desire to excel and persons with envy might enroll for evening or weekend classes to enhance their career for the sake of attracting recognition and other forms of reward. Such individuals might also work extra hours or do more work than they should in the belief that they will be recognized. For this reason, if you feel the urge to engage in unplanned career development and work extra hours to attract recognition and other rewards from your organization then you are probably envious. The major effect of envy is that it clouds your objective thinking and fixates your mind to particular things and people denying you the full experience.

Exercise

a. Give three situations in the recent past where you felt envious.

b. How did you overcome the envy?

c. What are the effects of envy that you experienced?

Worry or nervousness

Another common feeling at the workplace that is regarded as negative is feeling nervous or worried. For emphasis, feeling nervous is a welcomed as it is part of human feelings but like any emotion regarded as negative, it should be handled way to avoid creating an adverse impact on work relations and output. One of the ways you will notice when feeling nervous is that you become restless. If feeling worried, your mind is stuck on what could possibly go wrong and this elicits fear especially the worst case scenarios that replay on your mind. Expectedly, you will try to elicit multiple courses of action within a short period of time which only makes you more unease to the point that your uneasiness manifests in actions.

For emphasis, when feeling worried your mind wanders on the possible worst outcomes of the situation that is disturbing you. When worried you imagine the worst and rarely see the immense possibilities present. Think of being worried that your work contract might not be renewed. From this illustration, you are likely to feel nervous and start thinking of worst cases only where you are unable to pay house rent, service loans and kids and your wife are looking at you with huge disappointment. You are likely to be thinking of losing your social class and probably end up on the streets. Therefore, when one gets fixated on worst-case outcomes within a short period of time there are chances that he or she might be worried.

Thirdly, when feeling nervous you might want to excuse yourself from a meeting or conversation to be alone. One of the noticeable effects of being worried is that you might want a few minutes alone to recollect your mind and think through the situation objectively. If you get nervous in a meeting or during a conversation you might excuse yourself to go to the washroom or go back to your office cabin to calm yourself before resuming. For this reason, when you get the urge to be alone during a conversation or a meeting there are chances that you are feeling nervousness. Take the case of Grace who received a text that a foreclosure notice had been placed on her house while just about to start attending a meeting at work. She became sweaty and her heart pounded first and she did not trust how she would react so she excused herself and rushed to the washroom to think through the issue.

Fourthly, with a feeling of worry, you will talk to yourself or talk to objects to listen and assure you. When feeling worried, you are likely to talk to inanimate objects or engage in soliloquy to help you let out and think through the situation disturbing you. When an individual starts talking to himself or herself then chances are that the person is feeling worried. Like any other emotion, feeling worried is necessary to alert your mind and prepare it for any eventuality. However, the feeling becomes a concern when it begins overwhelming you or frequently recurs which will affect your productivity and relations.

Fifthly, when feeling nervous your nonverbal communication will give you away from such as trembling voice and avoiding eye contact. Another way of noticing nervousness is to pay attention to nonverbal communication that exhibits what a person might be masking. For instance, one might say that he or she is okay when the face is sweating, and the voice is trembling. The voice pitch of an individual who is nervous is likely to be high or low rather than the accustomed pitch. The gestures of an individual that is nervous are likely to be misaligned to their verbal message even though they are trying to project themselves as being in control of the situation. An individual that is worried might pace up and down frequently than he or she usually does.

Lastly when nervous you are likely to become self-conscious that everybody is aware you are unsettled and feel that they are judging you. In most cases, when one is nervous you are mentally aware of the state and try to compensate for the nervousness. As earlier on indicated, the society ridicules negative emotions forcing people to feel ashamed of manifesting such emotions and nervousness is one of the emotions. Feeling anxious is not the desired emotion and one is likely to feel that the audience or colleagues have noticed the negative emotions and are having a low opinion of the person.

Exercise

a. How do you handle nervousness when addressing an audience?

b. Why do you think society ridicules negative emotions instead of acknowledging them and seeking to safely express them?

Anger or aggravation

Anger might be one of the commonest negative emotions at the workplace and this is expected.

Workplaces have targets and evaluate their workers which create pressure and deadlines. When workers are under pressure and where the value is judged by defined expectations then they are likely to act under pressure. When one is pushed to the limit by deadlines then an individual may react impulsively by clicking, walking away or banging the table. Workers are also evaluated on the contribution to overall productivity and when workers feel the scoring system is not fair then they are likely to feel agitated. Anger can then be acknowledged as a negative emotion when one is unable to satisfy the expectations at an individual and public level.

Secondly, anger manifests as feeling highly offended. The reason for anger frequently manifesting at the workplace is due to the existence of diversity at the workplace where slight misconceptions are treated as deriding and degrading an individual. There are diverse workers in contemporary workplaces such as different sexual orientations, ethnicities, sexes and religious afflictions. What one might regard as normal communication and reaction might be offensive to others. For this reason, most contemporary might find offensive communication that another employee thinks is casual and harmless. Think of Richard who makes jokes that Muslims are oriented to violence without understanding that Ruth finds such casual talk offensive because one of her sons has converted to Islam. Ruth is really irked by the talk of Richard of Islam religion to the point of abandoning the tea break earlier than she does.

Furthermore, anger is exhibited as feeling insulted by the words or actions of a colleague. Another expression of anger is when one feels insulted by the actions or words. Such feeling is not necessarily linked to self-esteem issues rather lack of emotional intelligence by the person communicating. Mark is the leader of a team of five engineers at a local consultancy firm. Recently Mark suggested that nonperformers will be dropped and John felt insulted because he was rated low in the last appraisal. The feeling of being insulted aggravated to the point that John started considering terminating the contract to venture into business. In essence anger as an emotion is manifesting as a feeling of being insulted.

Similarly, anger is shown as feeling locked up by circumstances. When one feels that they have no options then it could be anger manifesting. If you are denied options or feel that you are not allowed alternatives then you will feel that you are under pressure. You will feel neglected and this form of anger. When you feel chained to processes that you have no control over you are likely to react by retreating to yourself or engaging in unjustified arguments. If you left with fewer options you are likely to feel cornered and undervalued. Restricted options might be misinterpreted to mean that you are not trusted and you are likely to feel insecure and scream at people at the slightest provocation.

Another way that anger is expressed is in the form of frustrations. When one feels the inability to control situations then anger is an expression of that frustration. As suggested when you feel cornered you are likely to feel no need to continue anymore. With frustrations, you will start disregarding the laid down procedures or become disconnected from your work. Feeling defeated will demotivate you and lead to a casual and unproductive approach to working. The other impact of frustration as a form of expressing anger is that you are likely to blame situations and other people rather than being accountable to yourself. In extreme circumstances, a frustrated employee might suggest that he or she does not care and mishandle customers especially when handling complaints.

Lastly, anger is manifested as sensitivity to negative feedback. The other form that anger manifests at the workplace is when one becomes sensitive to communication and actions. An individual that feels frustrated and undervalued by situations might become highly sensitive to the slightest hint of doubt or negative feedback. Such individuals quickly activate defensive mechanism by exploiting the conversation to play the victim card. When a person expresses anger as sensitivity to communication, he or she will invoke race, gender, sexual orientation, and religious affiliation to suggest that they are being discriminated against. The intent of being sensitive is to lock out others from fully exploring the issue at hand. In most cases, anger is an internal development and few people want to accept that they need help to enhance their emotional coping which makes sense as a way of locking up any conversation on the reaction.

Exercise
a. Anger is one of the common and negative emotions in the workplace. How do you cope with anger?

Dislike

Dislike is one of the negative emotions that is overlooked and sometimes misinterpreted to be something else. In this context, dislike refers to the general and unjustified feeling of disassociating and disinterest in someone or something. At one point you might have disliked someone or some movie character without any reason for feeling that. Dislike needs no justification just like love. Some dislikes are driven by social bias that eventually reinforces your personal bias. For instance, you might have just disliked the new worker even before you met or interacted. When you try to look for the reasons for disliking the innocent you do not get any. Dislike is a risk to developing social relationships as it denies you objectively assessing other individuals and this will affect your productivity as well as theirs.

Secondly, dislike manifests as stereotypes. Another way that dislikes manifests is in the form of stereotypes. If you have stereotypes against Latinos then you do not need any reason to dislike them, you only need to see or be told that the new colleague is a Latino. If you have stereotypes against women at the workplace then you only to meet one to dislike her. It is also important to acknowledge that you might develop stereotypes at the workplace even if you did not have one initially. Some of the dislikes are due to generalization. For instance, you might dislike the new intern from the University of Texas simply because the previous from the institution failed you at the workplace. For this reason, you do not need any reason to dislike the new interns as you have already developed a stereotype against the mentioned university.

Thirdly, dislike expresses as isolation. The other way that people express dislike is by isolating their targeted victims. Avoidance of meeting and involving the person you disregard is a way of expressing the feeling of dislike. The victim of the dislike might or might not notice the dislike. From this illustration, dislike costs mental energy as well as the overall productivity of the organization. If you harbor a dislike for an individual then you are likely to manipulate the composition of a team to push the individual away without taking into account the overall needs of the organization. Think of a new hire who is one of the few competent engineers in the new certification system but you dislike the new hire. You then go ahead and isolate the individual costing the organization of production.

Fourthly, dislike may manifest as a superiority complex. If you allow feelings of dislike to flourish then at some point you are likely to feel like the ultimate validation entity of what is good and what is not. The exhibition of feeling more important than others propagates dislike as a feeling. Essentially superiority complex is a contradiction of the intent of emotional intelligence competencies that seeks to advocate for consideration. In this manner, dislike is a confirmation of the likely low emotional intelligence of an individual. Take the example of Haron who feels that he is more qualified than everyone else at their company and feels that he understands better who should be hired and promoted. The company that Haron works for has promoted a colleague that Haron feels that the candidate is least qualified according to his sentiments but the organization thinks otherwise. While Haron is not jealous, he generally dislikes people he thinks are not up to his qualifications.

Fifthly, dislike may occur as justification. Sometimes dislike manifests as a justification. For instance, an employee may dislike another to justify his internal feelings. One might dislike others so as to feel valued and influential. Some people might show dislike to make other people seek to make peace with them which makes such individuals feel they matter. In a way, some people exercise dislike to help precipitate a crisis that enables them to exercise self-validation. For example, Richard dislikes Kevin but the goal of this behavior is to make Kevin seek ways to make peace with Richard. By having Kevin recognize that he needs to get along with Richard, the later feels valued in the organization.

Lastly, dislike can manifest as judgment. In some cases, the dislike of someone occurs due to the subjective judgment of the individual. When you judge someone by the first appearance as well as including any disability or physical features that you rate lowly then this is a judgment-driven dislike. The judgment of individuals is largely informed by stereotypes and past experiences. In judging people subjectively you classify them mentally and handle them based on that classification.

Exercise

a. Using initials only, list some of the people you dislike but cannot explain why you dislike them?

b. Which politician do you generally dislike; you have no reason for the feeling of dislike?

Disappointment or unhappiness

Disappointment like anger is a common negative feeling at the workplace. Feeling disappointed is unavoidable at the workplace due to needing to accomplish targets or fit in a certain circle. When a good intentioned worker fails to reach the set target or attain average score during appraisal then the person is likely to feel unhappy. The feeling is initially welcome as it can motivate the person to self-evaluate and commit to delivering more in the next cycle. Unfortunately, the feeling of being disappointed can persist and cause adverse effect to the self-esteem of the individual including negatively affecting the social life of the person. When you continuously feel disappointment you are also likely to express anger which might negatively affect your relationship with others.

Secondly, disappointment manifests as feeling let down. When one feels unhappy then the person is likely to feel betrayed by others. In most cases, disappointment arises when your expectations are not met and this can make you blame others for what happened. Think of an employee that was in a group and the entire group member contracts have been renewed except the one for the disappointed employee. Such a person is likely to lay blame on situations or other people for his unhappiness. Blaming others can lead to a new social problem especially where the person blames part of his family for disappointment at work. Think of an individual whose contract was not renewed but the person blames his wife for not being supportive enough during the period he was under probation which can create marital issues.

Thirdly, disappointment expresses as feeling not as good as others. When one is disappointed when the person is likely to feel inferior to others especially where others have excelled. Think of an employee whose contract was not renewed but those of others in the group were renewed. Such an employee is likely to feel that he or she is not as good as the others despite reassurances from the team. The reason for feeling inferior is that when one feels unhappy he or she is likely to blame oneself other than objectively navigating the circumstances that led to feeling unhappy. Remember our example, where only one member of the group failed to secure a new contract while others sailed through and the individual ended up blaming himself for the new status.

Fourthly, disappointment can manifest as not feeling appreciated enough at the workplace. As expected, if one is disappointed when the person might feel that his or her input is undervalued at the organization. It is difficult for a disappointed person to believe that the outcome was due to internal and external factors and not necessarily personal culpability. Finding somewhere to lay the blame is a way for your mind to reach some closure and restore mental status balance. Unfortunately, most people find it convenient to blame themselves other than identifying the factors that precipitated the disappointment. It is important that we unlearn the trained way of handling disappointment by learning not to blame ourselves for disappointment always.

Fifthly, the feeling of disappointment can show as avoidance. In some circumstances, disappointment might express as isolation where an individual that does not feel happy retreats to his or her world. Such a person might feel that by being alone, he or she will get time to reflect and design new strategies to improve in the next evaluation cycle. While brief retreat to your world is allowed, it can become problematic when you prolong the avoidance of social moments as this allows the negative emotions to reinforce each other. Think of our example where the single employee whose contract was not renewed in a group withdraws to his world and continues to blame everything including fate and entertains thoughts of quitting employment altogether.

Lastly, disappointment may manifest as increased need for validation. In most cases when one feels disappointed, then he or she might require affirmation that they are still as good as anyone else. Such individuals might engage in frequent submissions of reports or seek frequent feedback not because they want to improve but they want to get adequate positive feedback as a form of validation of their worth in the group. The need for validation is a confirmation that one is feeling disappointment especially in the case of a workplace after an appraisal report feedback. Disappointment in this context affects productivity by making the individual demotivated and engaging in unnecessary activities to help validate his or her worth to recoup from the unhappiness,

Exercise

a. How did you handle disappointment while in college?

b. How did you express your disappointment?

Chapter 4: Improving Emotional Intelligence

Emotional intelligence in the relationship

Notably, emotional intelligence will help each party in a relationship empathize more with one another. Empathy is one of the easily noticeable signs of emotional intelligence and concerns acknowledging and making a priority to the needs of the other person. Empathy is one of the components of a healthy relationship. In a way, empathy advocates for limited self-sacrifice to prioritize the emotional needs of the other party. The perception that the other person is involved in the conversation and is listening increases the feeling that one is valued. However, empathy does not imply that you totally forego your emotional needs in favor of the other party. The emphasis of empathy in a relationship is that it allows you to view the world from the other person's perspective which boosts mutual understanding.

Through emotional intelligence, one can initiate a critical conversation without it escalating. If you are emotionally intelligent then you are likely to process criticism safely. In a relationship, constructive criticism is necessary and it helps propagate the relationship. However, when criticism is not well received then it can shut down routine communication. Lack of communication is a significant danger to any relationship. Emotional intelligence can help prepare an individual to negative feedback and such a person is likely to be receptive to criticism. Some people are likely to react to criticism with anger and feeling judged. An individual with high emotional intelligence will welcome criticism with the understanding that emotional intelligence levels can be elevated to fix some of the shortcomings raised. Criticism in this context is treated as an avenue to recognize, learn and understand more your emotions and your actions.

Another criticality of emotional intelligence in a relationship is that it enables the parties to be fully vulnerable with one another. Being fully vulnerable to one another enables you to connect with one another. Most people are uneasy with being vulnerable to other people save for the one they trust. Emotional intelligence allows you to express your emotions fully including the negative emotions that you might not freely express in public. With emotional intelligence, you will acknowledge what holds you back including understanding how and when to manifest the emotions. The other partner will easily accommodate your vulnerability and view the world from your eyes due to exercising empathy which is a competence of emotional intelligence.

Expectedly, emotional intelligence competencies will enable you to express your feelings directly. Lack of emotional intelligence will force one of the partners to use passive aggression or silence to handle a conflict. Fortunately, emotional intelligence can help any aggrieved partner to explicitly express their feelings as well as be assertive. The understanding that all emotions are inevitable and should be expressed is enough to motivate one to manifest his or her emotions. In a context of emotional intelligence, all parties can manage to exercise empathy and this should make communication on issue direct. In this manner, emotional intelligence is a component of operationalizing honest in a relationship. Think of Janet who is feeling angry at Mark for not picking her calls all day and is confident that Mark understands why she is agitated. On the other hand, Mark empathizes with the way Janet is feeling and understands that the disappointment by Jane is not judging Mark and he does not take things personally.

Equally important is that emotional intelligence can help you apologize to each other and restore normalcy. One component of emotional intelligence is recognizing your emotions and being accountable. If each one of you acknowledges their emotions and assumes full responsibility for participating in the creation of that emotion and the subsequent reaction then it becomes easier to offer apologies when you offend the other. Another way that emotional intelligence can increase understanding by offering an apology is when an individual acknowledges and processes feedback from the other person. Emotional intelligence advocates for seeking views of other people about your emotions and corresponding reactions and utilizing the feedback to improve. Offering an apology is a way of acting on self-feedback and feedback from the other people in a relationship.

Lastly, emotional intelligence can help partners in a relationship recognize and solve a conflict. As indicated earlier on, conflicts are unavoidable due to each one of having different sets of values, views, and approaches to routine issues. With the increased diversity in relationships, conflicts are bound to happen frequently as well as due to increasing pressures of life such as high cost of living. With emotional intelligence, resolving conflicts becomes more practical as each party is willing to drop their hardline stance and process the issue from the viewpoint of the other party. If empathy flourishes, then the feuding parties are likely to soften hard stances and emphasis more on shared understanding enabling them to work towards a solution.

Exercise

a. In your previous relationship (friendship, work or romance) what caused the final disconnect according to you?

b. How could you have used emotional intelligence to resuscitate the failed relationship above?

Body language

Expectedly, body language is a critical part of emotional intelligence as it impacts empathy. Think of a colleague saying that he feels sorry for what you went through while smiling. Let us start with facial expressions as a form of nonverbal communication. Take note that the human face is highly expressive and can communicate countless emotions without verbalizing anything. Additionally, facial expressions tend to be universal unlike other forms of nonverbal communication. For instance, facial expressions for sadness, happiness, and fear tend to be universal. Most aspects of nonverbal communication are involuntary but with some coaching and practice, one can increase the alignment of facial expressions and verbal communication. At home, you can use a webcam to record random speech to see if the facial expressions and verbal communication. You can also try speaking about different emotions in front of the mirror to evaluate how your facial expressions align with your verbal expressions.

Another aspect of body language to watch out for is body movement and posture. Understand that people perceive you differently depending on the way you walk, stand or sit. For instance, if you are pacing up frequently while speaking to an audience then there are chances that you are hurrying the conversation or are feeling unease. Standing or leaning while listening or speaking shows that you are likely feeling tired or disinterested in the exchange. Slumping on the chair shows that you are feeling tired, distracted or disinterested in the conversation. If you are speaking to someone then the person is walking away then you are likely to view the person as showing rudeness or disinterest. Fortunately, body movement and posture as a form of nonverbal communication is highly controllable compared say to facial expressions.

Furthermore, gestures impact what you are communicating. The way you move your hands during communication constitutes gestures. Think of when you signal your friend to shut up, come or stop. When speaking with someone, the movement of your hands is sending their individual messages and you should try to align that message to what you are verbalizing.

Compared to body postures, gestures are not easily manageable as they involuntary reactions. Fortunately, through practice, one can improve the alignment of appropriate gestures and the intended messages. For example, when you throw up your hands in the air with quick succession while speaking, there is likelihood that you are offended. When you point using one of your fingers there is likelihood that you have judged the individual.

Similarly, eye contact is a critical aspect of nonverbal communication. Maintaining eye contact is critical to make the other person feel that you are interested in and are participating in the conversation. While keeping eye contact shows that you are actively participating in the conversation, sustained eye contact for more than one minute will distort the message as it amounts to staring or judging the individual. When speaking to an audience it is important to move your eye contact across the audience to avoid narrowing the nonverbal communication. Even though eye contact is nonverbal communication, it is important to acknowledge that some individuals were born shy and their lack of eye contact should not be misinterpreted to mean that they are disinterested or timid.

Additionally touch is a form of nonverbal communication. Even touch is not widely used but it is a form of nonverbal communication. Firm but gentle touch shows safety and care and this might be necessary for a romantic relationship and in parenting. The other common form of touch in public communication is a handshake. A firm handshake communicates confidence while a handshake that is not firm may communicate a lack of self-confidence. It is important to note that not all societies and individuals prefer handshakes. Even though handshake is a form of nonverbal communication, some people are born with medical conditions that make it difficult for them to shake hands such as an excessive palmar sweating condition known as hyperhidrosis. When processing handshake or lack of handshake allows some room for exceptions.

Then there is space which is a type of nonverbal communication. The physical distance between you and the other party in the communication is referred to as space. When you move very close to the other person, he or she might feel uncomfortable. However, for parties in a romantic relationship being closer physically might be the desired form of communication on some occasions. At the same time being significantly far from the person, you are communicating might suggest disinterest or casualness of the message. Being unnecessarily far from the person that you are communicating with might also increase distractions in communication. Think of when you are attending a workshop forum where the speaker sometimes moves close to your direction and goes back and stands at a distance that most people feel comfortable to listen.

Lastly, there is a voice as a form of nonverbal communication. The pitch of the voice communicates nonverbally. When the pitch of a voice is raised you are likely to process the message as anger or disappointment. An average level pitch will suggest that the speaker is settled and the emotional value of the message is within known limits. Similarly, a low pitch may suggest a lack of confidence, sorrow or discomfort of the speaker. However, it is important to understand that sometimes adjusting the tone is necessary to break the monotony, emphasize or show transition when communicating.

Exercise

a. How does tone affect the intent of communication?

b. Gestures and facial expression are among the most difficult forms of nonverbal communication to control. Do you agree with this assertion? Why or why not?

Active listening

Start by paying attention to the speaker and the message. Effective listening requires being in the mind and differentiating the message. Within an audience or any context of communication, there are multiple messages and exchanges and the ones that are needed are regarded as noise. For instance, people moving up and down, the wind blowing hard and phones ringing are communications but that which is regarded as noise. For this reason, an individual practicing active listening should selectively listen by focusing only on the speaker and the message conveyed. The other form of noise is internal and this includes diversionary thoughts and getting distracted by other thoughts. Think of feeling the urge to check social media updates while listening which is a form of internal distraction or noise.

Then show that you are listening through your body language and gestures. Communication is simultaneous and two-way and it is important that you reciprocate your listenership by expressing appropriate body language with respect to how the message is affecting you. Remember that the lead communicator relies on your reaction to adjust the communication for the benefit of everyone. For this reason, not communicating back is denying the speaker an early assessment of his delivery and the impact of his message. When listening actively, nod, clap and move your eye movements to help process the message and increase your focus on the communication. Think of revival churches' audiences' reaction to fiery preaching. Such audiences raise their hands, smile and nod actively.

Correspondingly, give feedback. One way of providing feedback is to politely interrupt and let the speaker repeat or capture your concern. The other way of giving feedback is to use nonverbal communication to make the speaker understand that you are receiving or not getting the intended messages. However, in most cases when one is not listening actively the feedback is involuntary such as slumping in the chair, staring at the roof or feeling disconnected from the audience and the moment. Some of the feedback constitutes bad listenership behavior such as seeking clarification from a colleague while the speaker is busy speaking. Both negative and positive feedback can be safely expressed using nonverbal communication.

It is important that you note down questions or areas that need clarification to avoid distracting your listenership. One of the issues that affect effective listenership is when an individual requires clarification and cannot get a chance to interrupt the speaker. For this reason, the individual allows the pending question to stay on the mind while timing for an opportunity to pose it to the speaker and this affects effective listening. One of the best ways to accommodate the need for clarification while effectively listening is to note down the question or area you need clarification and continue listening. By capturing the question on your notebook, you will free your mind and allow it to focus on developing communication.

Additionally, summarize what you listened. As you listen summarize the key points which allow your mind to internalize and connect the developing message. Noting the main points also helps you become mentally alert by connecting your body to the moment. While communicating, noise is everywhere in the form of colleagues whispering, phones vibrating, flickering lights and internal thoughts that deviate you from the message. Making an internal summary as well as a physical summary on your notebook or journal you increase your levels of concentration. However, it is important to understand that writing too much will affect effective listening. The goal is not to summarize but to listen and that is where you should focus.

Where possible, change position to get a clear projection of what is being spoken. Sometimes you might have to change your position where possible to get a clear view and voice projection of the speaker. Physical distance affects the efficacy of communication, especially where the audience is large and the projectors are absent. However, modern technology has improved large audience communication by using electronic projectors and sound public address systems to make voice projection and visualization of the speaker available at any angle. It is also not advisable to change seats during a speech as this might create unnecessary realignments and noise that might interrupt the speaker. A good practice is to arrive early enough or reserve a seat that will place you at a comfortable angle to receive and process the message from the speaker.

Exercise

a. How do you maintain attention when listening when having the urge to use your phone?

Mindfulness and relaxation techniques

There are six common mindfulness and relaxation techniques that are widely applied and one of them the breath focus. It is a simple but powerful technique where you take a long, gradual and deep breaths referred to as belly breathing. While breathing, try to gently disengage your mind from sensation and thoughts that distract you. The breath focus technique might useful for individuals with eating disorders to enable them to concentrate on their bodies in a positive way. Caution should be exercised for individuals with health-related breathing difficulties such as heart failure and respiratory elements. The technique of breath focus works by helping distract your mind from other thoughts and activities and this makes the mind perform a less costly task of breathing which helps ease your muscles and mind.

Additionally, there is another technique known as the body scan. In this technique, we mix breath focus with gradual muscle relaxation. Start with a few minutes of deep breathing then concentrate on one aspect of your body at a time and release any physical tension mentally. The value of body scan technology is that it can enhance mind-body connection awareness. Individuals that might find this technique useful are those from recent surgery and are grappling with body image issues. The body scan technique can be done independently or in a group setting. Additionally, the body scan technique can be accomplished by having an instructor guide you through the entire exercise. For this reason, this technique is highly flexible and costs less in terms of resources including time.

Another mindfulness and relaxation technique is guided imagery where one conjures up soothing places, scenes or encounters to help relax and focus. Fortunately, they are multiple applications on guided imagery. One of the impacts of guided imagery is that it can help reinforce a positive vision. The major weakness of guided imagery is that it can be challenging for persons having intrusive thoughts or persons that find it difficult to conjure up mental images. A suggestion of guided imagery is to visualize a staircase colored with all the rainbow colors and then walk or sit on each differently colored step. Then allow your mind to associate that color with positive natural sightings such as a lush green garden for the green colored step on the staircase. Using this repetitive and simple task, your mind will eventually delink from current costly thoughts and engage in this relaxing exercise.

Equally important, there is mindfulness meditation as a technique of mindfulness and relaxation. In this technique, one sits comfortably and concentrates on breathing as well as inviting your attention to the mind to the current moment. Our minds tend to wander into the past or future to help create continuity. Mindfulness meditation is likely to help individuals with depression, anxiety, and pain. The essence of this technique is to slow down the mind from being preoccupied with the future or the past. The mind controls us but in mindfulness and relaxation techniques we are trying to control it. Like any other form of meditation, one requires a calm place that is free from physical and electronic forms of distractions to successfully engage in mindfulness meditation.

Similarly, yoga is increasingly being used as a mindfulness and relaxation technique. Yoga involves a series of flowing movements where the physical aspects are expected to align with mental focus and distract the individual from continued thoughts. When feeling disturbed, it is a combination of emotional energy and physical energy that reinforce each other or rival each other which wears us out. With yoga, we harness both the physical and mental energy to calm the entire body. The other advantage of yoga is that it can improve flexibility and balance. In this way, yoga not only calms you but also exercise you. However, due to its physical cost to the body, yoga might be unfit for persons with certain health conditions. For this reason, yoga might be unreasonable to persons with pain or health problems that inhibit movements.

Lastly, saying repetitive prayer may help calm and focus the mind. For individuals that are irreligious, one can create a chant that helps the individual feel inner peace and calm. Saying repetitive chants reinforces the message to the mind and makes the mind believe or let go in line with the contents of the chant or prayer. It is important to understand that this technique might not work for everyone for it requires allowing your mind to travel to the message contained in the prayer or chant. One must also conjure up the ideal place or paradise when saying prayer or chant repetitively.

Exercise

a. Choose any two mindfulness and relaxation techniques and explain how you can implement them?

Chapter 5: Emotional Intelligence and Leadership

Good leadership

Emotional intelligence can enhance the honesty and integrity virtues of a leader. Through emotional awareness, a leader will get an opportunity to read his emotions and become aware of how he reacts to the emotions. At the same time, the leader will seek to take into consideration how other people are affected by the emotions of the leader. When communicating with others or when demonstrating something to the team, a leader will try to be as open as possible because he does not want others to feel disappointed by his dishonesty. In this manner, emotional intelligence is among the building components of an honest leader by making the leader aware of how others will react to his communication and actions.

Additionally, emotional intelligence can make a leader influential and inspire others. Through emotional intelligence, a leader will improve his or her communication and listening skills. For instance, emotional intelligence can enhance effective listening through empathy during a conversation. When speaking, a leader will appreciate the emotional value of each sentence and this will enhance the choice of words as well as the tone of speaking. When a leader shows empathy, actively listens, and speaks with consideration then the rest of the team is likely to feel respected and inspired. The other reason for the team likelihood of feeling inspired is to excel and get to display their leadership skills. It can be argued that emotional intelligence humanizes a leader from the viewpoint of those being led.

Furthermore, emotional intelligence can improve the commitment and passion of a leader. When a leader invokes emotional intelligence competencies to help understand the emotional needs of the team then the leader is showing commitment to helping improve the welfare of the employees. The determination to help others get the communication as well as not be affected by your emotions is an expression of passion and commitment to your role as a leader. Think of a leader who does not take critically the effect of his emotions and reactions to the team. Such a leader is likely to be viewed as disconnected to the realities of the workplace needs. Lastly, emotional intelligence allows a leader to get continuous feedback that can help enhance the passion to discharge leadership duties.

Another way that emotional intelligence can build a leader is by making the leader a good communicator.

As expected, effective communication is critical for a leader. Communication is the main avenue via which the leader delivers and receives an exchange of the message. There are nonverbal and verbal forms of communication and all of these forms need to reinforce each other. Communication is a science and art meaning that individually we can improve the communication to satisfy our message exchange needs. An individual that is open minded by dropping personal biases, and welcomes the views of others and at the same time pays attention to the effect of how he is communicating is likely to be effective in communication.

Equally important, is that emotional intelligence competencies improve decision-making capabilities of a leader. Decision-making capabilities require recognizing personal biases, overcoming impulses and regulating emotional reactions. In the absence of emotional intelligence competencies, one is likely to make impulsive and subjective decisions. Such decisions are largely ineffective as they are not based on the complete picture but rather what is convenient to the mind. Fortunately, emotional intelligence competencies resolve most of the shortcomings in decision-making by helping us actively acknowledge and discard stereotypes and ineffective communication. Imagine a leader who is not actively listening to suggestions or feedback during a brainstorming session. Additionally, you need emotional intelligence to effectively read nonverbal communication or nonverbal feedback regarding some of the decisions you want to implement.

Through enhancing the accountability of a leader, emotional intelligence competencies improve the appeal of a leader. For most people, they tend to avoid taking responsibility, especially where negative emotions are involved. Leaders not are tempted to blame situations or others instead of assuming full responsibility for what happened. However, by exhibiting emotional intelligence competencies, a leader will learn to process negative feedback without feeling like he or she has failed. One of the biggest reasons for not taking accountability by leaders and any other person is because it suggests that they are not competent enough to deliver. Stated differently, taking accountability increases chances of processing negative emotions and negative emotions are considered a weakness at the workplace.

Exercise
    a. In your own words, how does emotional intelligence and leadership connect?

Adaptation

One way that emotional intelligence can enhance leadership is through enhancing the flexibility of an individual during crisis situations. Leaders need to be adaptable because they cannot always control everything, especially external environment factors. High emotional intelligence implies that a leader is open-minded and can take different viewpoints other than the conventional one. Crises are unpredictable and require leaders to be open-minded. For example, through emotional intelligence, a leader will try to view the situation from the victims' perspective, from the organization's perspective, and from a personal viewpoint. Additionally, during a crisis, a leader will learn to process the volatile emotions from the victims as a way of expressing their anger and not necessarily to discount the leadership of the organization.

Secondly, managing work stress by invoking emotional intelligence can improve the influence of a leader. A leader has to guide the rest of the organization to new thinking and acting that the rest of the team might find difficult. If the leader is the only one adapting then the flexibility of the leader might not yield much. For this reason, a leader has to persuade others and dissuade fears of the team when trying new viewpoints and processes. A leader must convince others to trust his moves and this requires emotional intelligence. Persuading people requires one to understand their fears and this can be required empathizing with them including active listening.

Thirdly, emotional intelligence can enhance innovative solutions when handling problems. Part of being flexible requires thinking and acting creatively as some new circumstances require unconventional solutions. The ability to improvise is important for a leader. Take a case where a leader is rigid and this slows down the entire organization. Inflexibility might be a suggestion that a leader has a fixated mind which may correlate with persons that harbor and exercise stereotypes. Adaptability and creativity are likely to correlate with open-mindedness and this is a competence of practicing emotional intelligence. By taking into account different views of others as well as a personal view, a leader is likely to generate a creative solution.

Fourthly, emotional intelligence can enable a leader to handle unpredictable situations with significant success. One of the benefits of emotional intelligence competencies is that it can improve our anticipation and processing of negative emotions. One of the uneasiness with change and uncertainty is due to the fear of the unknown. Organizations have to take varied forms of risks such as embracing new technology, increasing affirmative action, and adjusting the business model. We all fear failure, stagnating, legal consequences and loss of status and for these reasons, human beings prefer status quo irrespective of its value. With emotional intelligence, one is likely to open up and welcome the possibility of negative emotions. In other terms, emotional intelligence is likely to make a leader a risk taker.

Fifthly, emotional intelligence can increase the adaptability of a leader by activating interpersonal competencies. Part of being adaptable as a person requires you to relate with others and this makes interpersonal competencies highly critical. A leader needs to disrupt the status quo and create a new equilibrium. During change, people are uneasy and emotional and it requires fine interpersonal skills to navigate the volatile environment and defuse tensions. Leaders must develop interpersonal skills which are essentially social skills. If you can recall, social skills are a derivative of emotional intelligence and a leader with social skills will exhibit effective interpersonal skills.

Lastly, emotional competence can enhance cultural adaptability of an individual. In the current workplace and the world, diversity is ever increasing and leaders require the flexibility of the mind. Leaders with emotional intelligence are likely to recognize and respect other cultures. While acknowledging and respecting other cultures appears easy, it is not easily implemented. Like most human beings, leaders are likely to view the world from the way they were raised which unfortunately includes stereotypes and personal biases. For this reason, a leader has to unlearn in order to become culturally competent. Most workplaces now have diverse workers in terms of ethnicity, religious affiliation, and gender among others. Our upbringing impacts the way we process issues to do with diversity and in grapevine communication, all people struggle to remain culturally sensitive.

Exercise
a. Luke is the team leader of engineers at Redline Consultancy, a startup that offers customization of cars. The company wants to change its current information system and this might necessitate retraining the employees as well as a reshuffling of employees. Using the adaptability competencies influenced by emotional intelligence, suggest three ways in which Luke can show effective leadership at the organization.

Leadership and performance

Through emotional intelligence leaders will acknowledge the impact of culture on productivity. Firstly, it is important that leaders connect leadership and performance of employees and indeed the organization. With good leadership, employees are likely to feel motivated and show commitment to the organization. One way of ensuring good leadership is to be an emphatic leader who listens and appreciates the team. A leader has to take the position of those he is addressing to understand their reaction and needs. The other way that emotional intelligence can help a leader make workers feel valued is social skills where a leader excels in interpersonal skills and leaves employees feeling respected and valued.

Additionally, motivated employees are likely to deliver. As indicated above, employees that feel valued are likely to attain set targets. Each one of us wants to value that we count and leaders play a significant role in making the team feel they matter. A leader needs to address the workers as a critical part of the organization and make it clear that the role of the leader is to occasionally refocus the energy of the team. Using communication techniques, the leader will help the employees feel they belong to the organization and when employees treat the organization like theirs, they tend to become accountable.

Furthermore, emotional intelligence application can help prevent conflicts in the workplace. Conflicts are unavoidable at the workplace. In the absence of leadership, conflicts will escalate and might lead to sabotage, employee turnover and in extreme cases violence. Leaders with emotional competencies will apply conflict resolution strategies to defuse tensions and restore normalcy. Good leaders will help individual workers gain and exercise emotional competencies and help lower chances of prolonging disagreements into conflicts. Without high emotional intelligence, leaders would inadvertently aggravate conflicts by appearing impartial or judgmental. For this reason, emotional intelligence enables the leader to defuse conflicts and sustain productivity in the workplace.

Through emotional intelligence, employees are likely to feel accommodated and deliver. Contemporary workplaces are increasingly becoming sensitive and leaders have to ensure that all workers feel safe, appreciated and accommodated. One of the common causes of leverage and friction is diversity. What one employee might consider as casual talk might turn out to be insensitive to the other employee. As the areas of diversity increase, so is the sensitivity of employees to verbal and nonverbal communication. The common areas of diversity include sexual orientation, gender, ethnicity, and religious affiliation. A leader is able to navigate the emotive issues and help employees understand their diversity and make everyone feel respected at the workplace.

Equally, important leadership helps make the team adaptable. Performance of an organization is also determined by how flexible the team is. Think of a team in an organization that is rigid and take significant time to adjust to the new business model or the newly installed system. The time spent to adjust costs the organization productivity. Good leadership ensures that the workers are flexible to ideas and approaches. The quality of flexibility is critical in helping the organization capitalize on changes in the market, especially technological changes. The leader is critical in helping shape the minds of the team in embracing changes at the organization.

For emphasis, good leadership helps communicate clearly the goals of the organization. Communication of targets and the ultimate goal is important to influence the attitudes and behaviors of the employees. A good leader will invoke emotional intelligence to ensure that the message communicated clearly. One of the ways of ensuring that the team understands the message is to employ empathetic speaking and active listening. It is also important the leader acknowledges the emotional value of words when communicating. Ineffective communication implies that the employees might not be having a shared understanding of the needs of the organization.

Finally, leadership helps elicit and act on feedback. Another critical element of productivity is extracting and acting on feedback and leadership offers an opportunity to capture passive and active feedback. There is always the feedback generated by the system but it is important to capture the qualitative feedback from the team itself concerning how they feel about the leader or the organization system. With this feedback, the leader should adjust communication and approach to maximize productivity in the organization. It is one of the overlooked areas in leadership and some leaders are not at ease with handling negative feedback. However, feedback is a critical aspect of continuous improvement.

Exercise
a. In your opinion, how does leadership relate to organizational performance?

The six styles of leadership

The first style of leadership is the visionary style and it concerns mobilizing people towards a vision. The visionary style works well when there is a clear direction or where change is required. For this reason, the visionary style of leadership is good where the climate is positive. The emphasis of visionary leadership is not reaching the specified place but rather getting everyone to embrace the vision. Another aspect of visionary leadership is that it advocates for autonomy and enables people to innovate and experiment to attain the set goal. In practice, failure when implementing visionary leadership is accommodated and employees feel comfortable experimenting in ways of moving the mission forward. It is important to have a clear mission that all employees acknowledge before attempting the visionary leadership style.

Secondly, coaching leadership style is another approach to leadership. The coaching style of leadership involves training employees to become better at what they do. It is important to acknowledge that there is a difference between coaching and micromanaging. The role of the manager in this leadership approach is to help employees evolve in their role and challenge the employees to surpass their assumed capabilities. In this approach to leadership, the manager grants employee's advice, tools, and support they require enabling them to succeed. However, coaching does not imply that the leader dictates what an individual will do at each step but instead directs them to attain the improved version of themselves.

Thirdly, there is the affiliative leader where the manager acts as an affiliate and makes connections in the entire organization. The intent of the affiliative style of leadership is to create a harmonious work environment where each employee knows and works well with each other. Expectedly, employees will not always get along and will disagree but this style of leadership seeks to fix that. The affiliate leader mends any broken trust in the organization. A leader can become an affiliative leader by developing a culture of recognition on the team. By building trust, the group will become closer and this will help build relationships.

Fourthly, democratic leadership is another common style of leadership. With the democratic leadership style, a manager will align a group towards an outcome. Democratic style of leadership is employed where the manager is not fully certain on the direction that the organization should take and the leader wants to leverage off the views and beliefs of the crowd to develop a clear path. The democratic style of leadership is critical when handling big decisions that might impact the future of the business. The motivation of the democratic style of leadership is the realization that collective intelligence is superior to individual knowledge.

Fifthly, there is a pacesetting leadership style. In this approach to leadership, the leader defines goals attainable without taking into account the feelings of the team. Pacesetting leadership places pressure on the team and exemplify what is required of the team. As expected, the pacesetting style of leadership has the risk of derailing the team and should be used with caution. It should be applied temporarily and for a short period. Sometimes a company has to expect much from its employees irrespective of the needs of workers and one of such situations include when the company is handling a crisis. One of the ways to attain results using this style is to balance this style with recognition.

Lastly, there is a commanding leadership style. In this approach to leadership, the leader invokes fear. The commanding style of leadership creates a perception of emotionless and cold. In most cases, the commanding leadership style evokes extreme negative effects on the culture of the company and is highly ineffective. The commanding style of leadership might only qualify during crises and it is not the best approach to show leadership during such times. The overall recommendation is to avoid using a commanding leadership style. For this reason, avoid ordering your team around and instead inspire participation as well as clearly explain the full situation. In conclusion, it is important to accept that there is no universal style of leadership and you might have to blend different styles of leadership depending on the situation you are facing. It is important to remember that you do not have to accomplish everything alone just because you are a leader as the team can always help with ideas. Empower your team to become leaders on their account and lastly develop emotional intelligence.

Exercise

a. Critique the commanding style of leadership.

b. Critique visionary leadership style.

How to improve

Start by recognizing the efforts of your team individually and collectively as a way of motivating the team. Acknowledging the contribution of your team is critical as it makes them feel valued and interested in group activities. Recognizing the contribution of your team is a form of reward and assurance that workers.

Some leaders might overlook the criticality of recognition as it is a psychological need. The recognition does not have to be formal always. For instance, you can offer positive remarks each time a team member submits a complete report on time. You can also use gestures or facial expressions to show satisfaction with the work of a team member. A leader has to show that he or she appreciates the effort of the team to make them feel they count.

Secondly, inform the team that the expectations are temporary and as a team, it is the ideal time to work together. When executing the command style of leadership or pacesetting style of leadership it is necessary that you furnish your team that the huge expectations are temporary to enable them to adjust and accept mentally the new demanding schedules. Sometimes a leader might be forced to hurry everyone especially during a crisis and under such circumstances; the leader might not allow democracy including understanding. In other terms, the leader might show less emotional intelligence competence when the sustainability of the organization is at stake. Under such circumstances, the leader has a duty to notify the workers why the environment has suddenly become stiff and burdensome to enhance their understanding and acceptability of the new approach of doing things.

Ensure to share the results of the efforts of the team on the bigger picture. In a typical organization, workers operate in a modularized manner. If not managed, the workers in each department might not have a comprehensive view of how they link to the entire organization productivity. For instance, the cleaners in an organization might not understand how they impact the success of the information technology department. A leader should seek to help individual teams understand how they collectively impact the entire productivity of the organization. For instance, cleaners ensure that the information technology department is organized and operate on time in a clean environment. The information technology department directly impacts the rest of the department.

Additionally, learn to trust your employees and improve your communication skills to enable you to freely discuss issues with anyone on the team. Without showing trust in your employees they will feel undervalued or they will feel that they are highly replaceable. If you trust your employees they will feel the urge to act responsibly as they are relied on to act independently. The absence of trust will make employees wait for supervision and deliver just enough to fulfill the contractual obligation. Trusting employees will also make them feel that they are part of the organization and are likely to take time to think of ways that they can help the organization improve.

Furthermore, offer suggestions to start a discussion on the project. Workers are sometimes reluctant to initiate a conversation, especially where such a discussion might appear to critique the leadership of the company. In such a case, it might help to initiate the conversation as a leader and encourage contribution from the team. In such circumstances effective communication especially aligning nonverbal communication to verbal communication is important. The tone of your voice, your facial expressions and gestures must speak one message to enhance the trust of the team. Before making any decisions, it is important to elicit as many views as possible and the people you are leading might have more effective solutions than you thought.

Lastly, consider all the ideas present and appreciate the contributors. As a leader, you will frequently engage with team members and it is important to acknowledge and appreciate each opinion floated. Leaders that do not appreciate the contribution of each member risk having diminished contribution in the subsequent meetings. Using words such as thank you, noted, appreciated and using nonverbal cues such as nodding, smiling and clapping shows that you are listening and appreciating the contribution of each member present. A leader should make a decision using the best suggestions available but show that he or she has listened and will save the other suggestions for future use.

Exercise

a. Have you ever held a leadership role? If no, think of a movie character that holds a leadership role. How did the leader show growth or improvement in executing his or her mandate?

The five components of emotional intelligence in leadership

The first component is self-awareness and it impacts leadership in several ways. Individuals that are self-aware understand how they feel and have knowledge of how their emotions will impact other people. As a leader having self-awareness implies that you know your strengths and weaknesses as well as portraying as a humble individual. You can operationalize self-awareness in leadership by slowing down your emotional reaction. Imagine if a leader that is quick to react and bang the table when irritated. It would become difficult to disagree with such a leader and one is likely to conform to the demands of such a leader to avoid confrontation. Additionally, self-awareness helps a leader become an effective communicator by understanding how the audience is feeling due to what he or she is communicating.

Secondly, there is self-regulation as an emotional intelligence component in leadership. Each one of us gets the urge to react impulsively as it is the most natural way of expressing and acting on the emotions. Self-regulation relates to the tendency to stay in control and avoid letting emotions guide you. Self-regulation does not imply that one is locking up their emotions rather one is exerting control on the reaction to the emotions. Leaders with self-regulation competency avoid impulse reaction to emotions such as verbal attacks when someone offends them. I will urge to watch the late Koffi Annan who was a former Secretary General of the United Nations and how he handles criticism during meetings or press conferences. Intense emotions and impulse reactions derail the mind of the leader.

Correspondingly, you can enhance your self-regulation through understanding your values. A set of personal rules and personal philosophies constitute personal values. With your individual code of ethics, you will inform your mind of its limits irrespective of the situation. It is also important to hold yourself accountable. The tendency of blaming others is an escapist approach to handling challenges and personal weaknesses. When you assume responsibility for your actions then you are granting yourself a chance to examine and fix your shortcomings. Lastly, it is important to practice staying composed when facing a challenging situation. You can breathe deeply and assure yourself that you will not let the negative emotion overwhelm you.

Thirdly, motivation as a component of emotional intelligence is integral in leadership. Leaders that are self-motivated will work consistently to achieve goals. Such leaders will also show high standards for the work they churn out. One of the ways that one can improve self-motivation is by reexamining the purpose of signing up for the position. Sometimes, people forget what made them take up the opportunity to work and by reflecting on why you took up the opportunity you might reignite your passion for the job. Beginning with what spurred you to assume the role might help you realize the commitment you need to show as a leader.

Then there is empathy as an emotional intelligence element that is expressed in effective leadership. Empathy is one of the critical elements of emotional intelligence and leadership. It is the ability to place yourself in the place of others to understand them better. Leaders with empathy are regarded as understanding, approachable and human compared to those that do not. A leader may show empathy by understanding why the members are unease with the new regulations or why employees are calling for several meetings before they embrace the new changes. With empathy, a leader will not feel disrespected or hated by the team members when communicating newer demanding changes.

For emphasis, contemporary workplaces are striving to be as humane as possible. Leaders that show empathy earn respect and loyalty from the team. When employees speak, try to abandon your position and view the world from the employees' eyes. Being empathetic does not imply that the leader is indecisive. One of the ways of improving empathy is to pay attention to the body language of the speaker and respond to the feelings. Some employees might use nonverbal cues to communicate their fears and disappointments and the leaders must read and respond to these.

Lastly, there are social skills that manifest in leadership. One of the ways of applying social skills in leadership is in conflict resolution. Expectedly, social skills rely on effective communication and active listening. With social skills, a leader will handle and solve conflicts diplomatically. In the absence of social skills, a leader might aggravate conflicts and lead to employee turnover, sabotage and even violence at the workplace. Fortunately, leaders can learn to become polished conflict resolvers and enhance their communication. An emotionally intelligent leader will easily recognize the shared ground of the feuding parties by reading their emotions when certain issues are mentioned and build on the common ground to cultivate a solution.

Exercise
   a. Look for one episode of the TV series House of Cards and judge the emotional intelligent competencies of Kevin Spacey? Do you agree or not with his manipulations?

Social skills

One of the skill sets needed for emotional intelligence is survival skills. The specific competencies here include the following guidelines, listening, ignoring distractions and using brave talk as well as rewarding yourself. Social contexts might require you to follow instructions and overlook distractions. Not all people can ignore distractions as the human mind processes everything it can decipher. It is important to train your mind to act in a disciplined manner by avoiding distractions and sticking to the recommended guidelines. It is also important that you reward yourself to enable you to feel worth engaging in social interaction.

The second sets of skills needed in socially competent individuals include interpersonal skills. The particular skills here include asking for permission, sharing, waiting your time, and joining an activity. It takes the experience to know when to interrupt or join a conversation. In most cases, the range of required interpersonal skills depends on the context. The argument here is that the interpersonal skills you exercise when watching your favorite team play are not the same as the one you exhibit when with your colleagues at the workplace.

The third skill sets regarding social skills include problem-solving skills and specifically asking for help, accepting consequences, and apologizing. In social contexts, disagreements will occur and at the same time, the parties in the interaction might require your input to resolve an issue. A socially competent individual needs to identify the underlying causes of the problem, how it is affecting others, why the rest of the people are feeling the way they are, and finally offering impartial and multiple ways of fixing it.

The fourth skill sets include conflict resolution skills and specifically handling loses, accusations, peer pressure, and dealing with flatter. Resolving conflicts is a highly demanded skill in contemporary society that is increasingly diverse. Solving conflicts require being impartial, empathically listening and helping the feuding parties acknowledge their shared ground on the issue. Unresolved conflicts can end social interactions and at workplace affect productivity in several ways. For instance, unresolved conflicts can make some workers quit a certain team or leave the organization altogether.

The fifth aspect of social skills concerns the ability to persuade and influence others. In social contexts, one should possess the ability to convince others. Influencing others relies on emotional intelligence competencies especially empathy and emotional value communication. When you understand the emotional impact of the words in your communication then it becomes easier to use it to win others. Persuading people also means that you appreciate how they feel and take into account when communicating with them.

The sixth sets of skills for the socially competent individual include leadership skills. Within social contexts, sometimes one has to show leadership. Within a group, it will require a leader or a dominant member and possessing leadership skills is part of social skills. A good leader inspires and listens while being visionary. When participating in social contexts, it is important that you cultivate leadership skills and demonstrate them where appropriate. One of the preferred models of leadership is the transformative leadership where the leader motivates the members rather than commanding or setting the pace for the team.

Equally important is communication skills that operationalize social skills. As expected, communication skills are essential in any social activity. Some of the communication skills required includes effective use of nonverbal communication. It is important that the facial expressions and gestures used are appropriate and at the same time tally with the verbal communication. Groups are likely to be diverse and hand gestures might have different connotations for each member involved. For this reason, communication should also include cultural competencies.

Furthermore, building bonds is requisite for social skills. Part of social interactions is developing relationships. Creating a relationship will also require a skill to sustain the relationship. Not all people can initiate and sustain a relationship. The competence of building and sustaining relationships is part of the social skills that one must possess. Empathy is a critical competence when building and managing a relationship. Building and handling relationship is largely an art but following best practices increases chances of succeeding

Finally, change management skills are a critical part of social skills. Another continuous aspect of social interactions is changing. In any group setting, one or several members might leave or behave differently than the known behavioral set and these calls for change management competencies to avert fallouts in the group.

Exercise

a. Use a past experience, explain how some of the social skills were exhibited or not exhibited.

Conclusion

In summary, the author managed to take the reader through want is emotional intelligence and how it differs with other related concepts such as social intelligence and emotional intelligence. The author provided an exercise at the end of each chapter to enable the reader to reflect. The exercises are easy to do and at most involve only two questions. Using easy and relatable examples, the author hopes to make the reader realize that emotional intelligence is manifesting in and around us. The approach of the author on the topic is from a neutral point of view and this lets the reader make a judgment on the suggested value of emotional intelligence.

Finally, this book weaves together what would be separate books on emotional intelligence making this book an interpreted approach to emotional intelligence. Throughout the book, the author maintains the simplicity of language and pays attention to the applicability of the suggested areas of emotional intelligence to the workplace, individually and social events. The content of the book has been carefully evaluated to ensure that is relevant and applicable in all contexts. Against this backdrop, this book can be seen as a manual and personal assessment of applicable emotional intelligent for individuals and groups.

If you found this book useful in anyway, a review is always appreciated.

Empath – A Complete Healing Guide

Self-Discovery, Coping Strategies, Survival Techniques for Highly Sensitive People. Dealing with the Effects of Empathy and how to develop to Enhance Your Life NOW!

By Ewan Miller

Table of Contents

Emotional Intelligence – Life Mastery
Table of Contents
Introduction
Chapter 1: Understanding Emotional Intelligence

    Emotional intelligence versus intelligence quotient
    Emotional intelligence versus social intelligence
    Emotional intelligence in psychology
    A brief history of emotional intelligence
    Other research and studies on emotional intelligence
    Emotional intelligence framework
    High and low emotional intelligence
    Why developing emotional intelligence is crucial
    Self and relationship management
    Emotional intelligence in the workplace
    Emotional intelligence and relationships

Chapter 2: The Application of Emotional Intelligence

    Handling Impulses
    Handling difficulties and setbacks
    Handling stress and anxiety
    In the workplace
    Coping with trauma
    Coping with reactions

Chapter 3: Recognizing Emotions

    Envy
    Worry or nervousness
    Anger or aggravation
    Dislike
    Disappointment or unhappiness

Chapter 4: Improving Emotional Intelligence

    Emotional intelligence in the relationship

Body language
Active listening
Mindfulness and relaxation techniques

Chapter 5: Emotional Intelligence and Leadership

Good leadership
Adaptation
Leadership and performance
The six styles of leadership
How to improve
The five components of emotional intelligence in leadership
Social skills

Conclusion

Empath – A Complete Healing Guide

Self-Discovery, Coping Strategies, Survival Techniques for Highly Sensitive People. Dealing with the Effects of Empathy and how to develop to Enhance Your Life NOW!

By Ewan Miller

Table of Contents
Introduction
Chapter 1: What is an Empath?

Are You Empathic or an Empath?
How Does It Feel to Be an Empath?
Most Common Traits of Empaths
Born Empaths vs. Learned Empaths
Are You an Empath? QUIZ

Chapter 2: The Empath's Peace of Mind and What Hinders It

Common Problems as an Empath
The Narcissist and the Empath
What Are "Energy Vampires"?
Downsides to Being a Powerful Empath

Chapter 3: The Gift of Being an Empath

    The Benefits of Being an Empath
    Self-Awareness and the Awareness of Others
    Healing and Helping Others
    Possible Professions to Help You Thrive in Life as an Empath

Chapter 4: Healing and Balancing Tools for the Empath

    What Are Spiritual Healing Tools and How to Use Them
    Energy Clearing for the Self and Others
    Awareness and Mindfulness Practices
    Steps to a Grounding and Balancing Meditation

Chapter 5: How to Keep Unwanted Energy from Influencing You as an Empath

    When Other People Are Negative: Ways to Protect Yourself
    Grounding: Before and After
    Communicating Boundaries

Chapter 6: Quality Space and Time

    Why You Should Limit Time with Other People or Groups
    Space and Time for Reflection and Rejuvenation
    Relationships and the Empath

Chapter 7: How to Avoid Empathic Burnout

    Guidelines for Maintaining Balance and Stability
    Applications to Aid You in Times of Stress or Burnout

Conclusion

⊠ Copyright 2019 by Ewan Miller - All rights reserved.

This content is provided with the sole purpose of providing relevant information on a specific topic for which every reasonable effort has been made to ensure that it is both accurate and reasonable. Nevertheless, by purchasing this content, you consent to the fact that the author, as well as the publisher, are in no way experts on the topics contained herein, regardless of any claims as such that may be made within. As such, any suggestions or recommendations that are made within are done so purely for entertainment value. It is recommended that you always consult a professional prior to undertaking any of the advice or techniques discussed within.

This is a legally binding declaration that is considered both valid and fair by both the Committee of Publishers Association and the American Bar Association and should be considered as legally binding within the United States.

The reproduction, transmission, and duplication of any of the content found herein, including any specific or extended information will be done as an illegal act regardless of the end form the information ultimately takes. This includes copied versions of the work physical, digital, and audio unless express consent of the Publisher is provided beforehand. Any additional rights reserved.

Furthermore, the information that can be found within the pages described forthwith shall be considered both accurate and truthful when it comes to the recounting of facts. As such, any use, correct or incorrect, of the provided information will render the Publisher free of responsibility as to the actions taken outside of their direct purview. Regardless, there are zero scenarios where the original author or the Publisher can be deemed liable in any fashion for any damages or hardships that may result from any of the information discussed herein.

Additionally, the information in the following pages is intended only for informational purposes and should thus be thought of as universal. As befitting its nature, it is presented without assurance regarding its prolonged validity or interim quality. Trademarks that are mentioned are done without written consent and can in no way be considered an endorsement from the trademark holder.

Introduction

An Empath is someone who has the capacity to feel what other people feel. Have you ever been sitting in a room with someone, and without words, you just knew what happened to them at work that day? Have you ever had an experience where you left a party at a friend's house, and you felt depressed and unworthy without knowing why? When you spend time with others, does it change the quality of your emotions or thoughts in a significant way? Are you able to pick up on other's concerns, fears, doubt and worries before they even tell you what they are?

If you answered yes to these questions, then you are most likely an Empath. Many people confuse being an Empath with being empathic; however, there is a great difference. To be an Empath, you must accept that you are not just an empathic person or friend and that you are more open to relating to someone else's personal feelings through receiving their emotional energy directly.

We are all energy, and our system of energy is always throbbing and pulsing with how we think, feel, react, and respond. Empaths are highly sensitive to the energy of others, but it doesn't mean they are highly sensitive emotionally. This can come as a surprise to any Empath who has always been told they are "too sensitive" or "too emotional."

An Empath is neither of these things; they are simply attaching to the feelings of others more easily than they understand or realize. If you think you may be an Empath, this book is for you. If you have had a long life of taking on the cares, worries, fears, and concerns of others on a deep and intense level, then you need to read this book.

There are a lot of tools, tricks, and guidelines within these pages to help you find a good balance and keep your energy clear so that you are not collecting and keeping the unwanted energy of others. This book will offer explanations and understandings about what can be troublesome as an Empath, and also what a gift and benefit it is to your life.

Throughout these pages, you will find all of the resources that you will need to understand, embrace, and healthfully walk the path of the Empath. So, what are you waiting for? Begin your journey today!

Chapter 1: What is an Empath?

As you begin to discover more about the world of the Empath, it is important to gain a clear understanding of what makes some people this way. How do you become an Empath, or are you born with this gift? What makes someone an Empath or just an empathic person?

In this chapter, you will learn what the most common traits of the empath are, how it feels, and what it can look like. We are always looking for an answer to our questions, and this chapter will help you understand how to identify if you or someone you know is an Empath.

As you read with an open mind, be prepared to unlock some of your own answers to your life questions. You may find that you were an Empath all along, and you just weren't sure how to identify your experience. Having a clear understanding of what it feels like or how it manifests in your daily life can help you achieve the knowledge to claim your unique gift and live in harmony with it throughout your life.

Are You Empathic or an Empath?

So, what's the difference? How can you be an empathic person and not be an Empath? Aren't they the same thing? There is a big difference between the two. To be an empathic person, all you need is the ability to understand someone else's feelings. When you are with your friends, family, or colleagues and they share something profoundly emotional, you may be able to relate to their experience empathically or simply to understand where they are coming from and share your empathy for their situations.

An Empath will physically and emotionally sense and feel the experience of the other person. This is quite different from simply understanding someone's emotional expression that they verbally communicate to you. An Empath will be able to understand the feelings of another by actually feeling them as well, and this can become a lot like taking them on as though they are your own.

Many people who are Empaths and don't know how to work with their gift, come home at the end of the day feeling exhausted, low-energy, sad or depressed, and unable to express their own true feelings because they have picked up on the emotions of so many others through the grind of the day.

The unwanted emotions of others can cling to the energy of the Empath because of how open and receptive they are to sensing, feeling, and attracting those energies and feelings. If you are simply empathic, then you will not have the same kind of experience that an Empath will. You may feel like a good friend or coworker because of your ability to hear someone's experience and offer them compassion and empathy, but you are not an Empath unless you are sensing and feeling someone else's emotions or feelings without verbal communication. It is an energetic knowing on a deeper level that sets the Empath apart from the empathetic.

How Does It Feel to Be an Empath?

Understanding the difference, you can now determine how it may feel to have these kinds of experiences. To many Empaths, there is no way to determine how they are being affected by others until they learn how to work with their gift and accept that they are Empaths in the first place. If you know you are an Empath, then you will be better able to understand how to care for yourself, as well as others, without affecting your own emotional state to the detriment of your life experience.

When you are aware of your Empath skills, you may already have an acquaintance with some of these side effects, and if you are just learning how to identify your gift, then the following list may help you discover if you have been an Empath all along without even realizing it.

<u>*How It Feels to Be an Empath:*</u>

- Sensitivity to loud noises, scents or aromas, bright lights, and other impactful stimuli

- Headaches on a regular basis

- Frequent colds, sinus problems, or "allergies"

- Emotional or mental burn out

- Exhaustion or chronic fatigue

- Emotional highs and lows for no obvious reason

- Care-taking of others as a way of living; the natural nurturer

- Depression, anxiety, paranoia, and fear for no obvious reason

- Sensing something before it has actually happened

- Feelings of discomfort after entering someone's home, office, or other buildings

- Insomnia or difficulty sleeping

- Indigestion or other stomach discomforts

- Hypersensitivity when someone feels angry, hurt, scared, or depressed

- A constant need to feel something other than what you have energetically acquired from others (example: alcohol, drugs, sweets, snacks, etc.)

- Confusion and disorientation after being in large crowds

- Feelings of anxiety after being in large crowds

- Mental and/or emotional discomfort after spending "quality time" with certain people in your life

- Easily distracted by unwanted feelings of others

- And the list goes on, but you get the picture...

So many of these symptoms or side effects seem like common physical or psychological issues that can be healed by a physician or a therapist. However, if you are an Empath, these side effects are the direct result of acquiring the emotional energy of other people everywhere you go and with everything you do.

You may not have realized it your whole life, but the reason you have a chronic illness and can never sleep is that you have taken on so many different people's feelings and carried them with you. It is important to understand how strong and powerful emotional energy can be. This list can demonstrate that truth. Emotional energy is so powerful that it can cause these types of problems for the Empath, but also the person experiencing the emotions.

There are also positive expressions of how it feels to be an Empath, especially when one is grounded and balanced:

- Uplifted and energized

- A sense of purpose

- Joy for helping others

- Deep understanding of more than just an emotional level

- Self-awareness to a great degree

- Awareness of others to a great degree

- Psychically/Spiritually open

- Connected to all things in general

- Warm and happy

- Able to understand more than what is seen or said

As an Empath, you can go both ways, either feeling a great many of the difficult and challenging aspects of having this gift or experiencing the more uplifting and high vibrational energetic qualities of being such an open source of love and understanding. Imbalance in our own feelings and emotions can be a source of great trauma in the life of the Empath.

When we are unbalanced with ourselves, our bodies, minds, and hearts seek to communicate with us and let us know when something is off. This is a powerful thing to know for an Empath, especially. If you are experiencing certain side effects or symptoms, it may be your body and mind telling you that you have taken on too much of someone else's energy and you need to clear that energy and ground yourself back into a balance and harmony with your own being.

To further help you understand what an Empath is, let's look at some of the more common traits that they possess.

Most Common Traits of Empaths

For many, the Empath is no more than just a regular, everyday man or woman who has a higher emotional expression or a better way of sensing or "seeing" someone else through their gift of empathy. However, a true Empath can exhibit even greater gifts and abilities that might seem common but certainly, are among the world of Empaths.

There are several traits that only manifest after you have spent time and energy, clearing out any blockages or congestions of energy in the system and can be very pronounced or very subtle. Other traits are fairly noticeable and common for an Empath regardless of whether they are grounded and balanced. The most common traits can be found in the list below:

- Highly Intuitive

- Often Introverted

- Easily senses lies or deceit quickly

- "Predicting" future events (sensing them)

- Receiving Input from others in the form of energy (emotional, mental, physical, and sometimes, spiritual)

- Ability to sense or "know" when something is "off"

- Highly creative

- Naturally inquisitive

- Absorbs the feelings and emotions of others easily

- Natural caregiver or nurturer

- Forgiving and selfless

- Urge to make things better or "right"

- Proclivity for seeking fairness

Some other traits that may not be considered common are also a part of being a well-developed and grounded Empath:

- Clairvoyance- clear seeing

- Claircognizance- clear knowing

- Clairsentience- clear physical knowing

- Clairaudience- clear hearing

- Clairempathy- clear emotional feeling (sensed in others and the self)

- Psychic openness and ability

You may find that you possess other traits not listed here that may be directly related to your abilities as an Empath. Keep in mind that this is a simple list of the more common traits of the Empath and that they are more than can be experienced. If you are an Empath, then you are highly intuitive and will be able to clearly discern other elements of your own journey and experience that are linked to your gift.

Born Empaths vs. Learned Empaths

We all have the capacity and ability to become Empaths. Some people are naturally inclined to become this way because of their innate personality or how they were raised. Others may have a desire to become an Empath and practice learning how to open themselves to these skills. It is possible either way; let's examine how these two experiences are different and also how they are alike.

A born Empath is likely someone whose entry into this world has a specific purpose or profession that they needed to align with. A person who has always been naturally skilled at the art of nurturing, healing or caregiving may have likely been an Empath at an early age and was already practicing and honing in on this quality about themselves, though it is unlikely they had a name for it.

If you were an Empath growing up, it is likely that you never knew it. Most people are not aware of their gift at an early age, and it can cause a lot of problems due to a lack of understanding and knowledge about why they are considered more sensitive than others or why they have difficulties with school or social activities.

Often times, a person learns to become an Empath when they are young due to a family dynamic. Depending on how you were raised, what kind of household dynamic you learned in or how your parents acted or reacted emotionally in their partnership or their relationship with you, it could have started your journey as an Empath, giving you an unconscious reason to become more perceptive and intuitive as a means of survival or acceptance in your family or culture. So, even if you weren't born an Empath, you could have developed this skill at an early age without knowing it at all.

These early life Empaths struggle in culture or society and even in their own homes as adults, especially if their gifts were never nurtured or identified leading to difficulties in romantic partnerships, jobs, and other relationships, as well as issues with drugs, alcohol, or other addictions to help relieve the stress of being an unidentified Empath. Some people who are Empaths at an early age thrive well because their parents or caregivers are responsive to their abilities and needs and can help them develop their skills in a positive way.

Learned Empaths are those who can become Empaths naturally, as in the above example of childhood conditions and modeling, or through study and practice. Many people have a desire to expand their ability to be more receptive and sensitive to the needs of others and seek to learn how to open their energy up to become better able to "read" the emotions of others. This could be out of a desire to help people or improve relationships or assist with a profession that requires a lot of empathy.

Most of the time, true Empaths are those that are innately carrying this tendency as they enter the world, and have a life purpose to fulfill or have it learned as a child due to family dynamics. Oftentimes, Empaths do not discover their true nature until they have begun to grow into adulthood and learn to examine more deeply their interpersonal relationships, cultural and societal experiences, and personal family dynamics.

When you ask yourself whether or not you are an Empath, look back on your early life and your growth experience. How did you relate to your family and others? Do you still relate to them in this way? Take the following quiz to determine whether or not you might be an Empath.

Are You an Empath? QUIZ

1. Do I find myself alone often to feel at peace?

2. Do I get overwhelmed easily in large groups or crowds?

3. Have I been called "too emotional," "too sensitive," or "too shy"?

4. Am I able to spend time with others for long periods of time without feeling anxious or drained?

5. Am I sensitive to loud noises, bright lights, or excessive stimuli?

6. Am I sensitive to aromas, perfumes, and odors?

7. Do fights and arguments make me feel physically ill?

8. Do I feel drained by other people?

9. Would I consider myself introverted?

10. Do I tend to use food, drugs, or alcohol to cope with things?

11. Am I frequently anxious or worried?

12. Do I have difficulty sleeping?

13. Do I need a long period of time to rest or recuperate after being around certain people?

14. Do I prefer to have an easy out if I am at a party, like bringing my own car, or having an excuse ready for when I want to duck out early?

15. Do I prefer to be alone rather than engage in emotionally-taxing relationships?

16. Am I happier with intimate, one-on-one discussions, or large group dynamics?

17. Am I sensitive to prescription drugs or over the counter medications?

18. Do I have a tendency to get sick often, with colds, allergies, or sinus infections?

19. Are there people in my life that make me feel worse after talking to them?

20. Are there times when I feel like I need to be far away from people and cities in order to recover my energy?

21. Do I have emotional discomfort frequently?

22. Can I sense when the energy in the room has changed because either someone entered the room or left it?

23. Do other people's problems keep me awake at night?

24. Am I overwhelmed by complicated tasks that require multi-tasking?

25. Do I feel exhausted all of the time?

If you answered yes to at least 20 of these questions, then you are an Empath. Consider each answer and go with your first instinct. People are always looking for the right answers to these questions, but the right answer is how you find out whether or not you need to follow your path as an Empath or not. The odds are that if you are reading this book, then you already suspect that you know you are an Empath and that you need to know how to develop your skill and gift.

Throughout the rest of this book, you will learn how Empaths struggle, how they ground and balance, and what to do to help yourself align with your ability so that it works FOR you and not against you.

Chapter 2: The Empath's Peace of Mind and What Hinders It

As you read in the last chapter, there are circumstances and relationships that can have a powerful impact on the quality of life of the Empath. Everyone wants a little peace of mind, and for someone who absorbs the emotional and mental reflections of those around them, centeredness of the mind can be hard to come by.

There are a lot of ways that these issues can manifest for the Empath. This chapter takes a deeper look at identifying some of the more common ways that you can be afflicted by the negative or unwanted emotions of others. As you read, take of note of any of the situations or personalities that might currently be affecting your own energy and emotional well-being.

Common Problems as an Empath

If you took the quiz in Chapter 1, then you have already identified some of the common problems that the Empath can face. The problems of the Empath beget the traits of the Empath. Essentially, much of what creates an energetic or emotional disturbance for an Empath results in the way they choose to live their life: often introverted, happier alone or in small groups, away from crowds, and sensitive to experiences.

Let's take a look at the following list of some of the more common problems that an Empath can face when they are not in command of their gift:

- Frequent Illness- this is not always true for an Empath, however, if you are not in a good balance or grounded in your ability, then you have a tendency to absorb other people's energy and too much of too many different people's feelings can lead to a depleted immune system causing more availability to fall ill.

- Patterns of Guilt, Anxiety, and Depression- Many Empaths, without knowing it, linger within these feelings as the result of being TOO open and available to the sensations and feelings of others, resulting in another person's depression becoming a part of your energy to the point that you can't identify whether it belongs to you or someone else.

- An Easy Target- Empaths have a way of attracting people who need a shoulder to cry on. They are naturally good listeners and have a tendency to help people feel better when they are feeling low or blue. What the Empath can take away are those low, blue feelings, or a feeling of exhaustion or being drained after such an encounter.

- Isolation- Many Empaths find that they feel most at peace when they are alone in the comfort of their homes where they can live with their own energy. Empaths may be introverts, but they still need human interaction and so finding a balance between finding sanctuary alone and being with people can be a problem for an Empath.

- Unpredictable Highs and Lows- A true Empath will always have to protect themselves from other people's energy, and when they don't, they will find that they bring other people's ups and downs into their life on a frequent basis. From the interaction with the disgruntled cashier to the angry parent on the playground, from the joyful and friendly postal worker who makes your day, and then back home, you will be absorbing the potent energy of others throughout the day through your interactions. This can stimulate a wide range of highs and lows that can make your head spin if you are not fully grounded and in awareness with your gift.

- Exhaustion- all of the energy you receive and don't let go of gets trapped in your energy field and keeps you vibrating on a lower level. The only way to get rid of other people's energy is to clear it away from yours (more on that latter), and if you don't take the time to either ground yourself first, or clear yourself after, or both, you will end up feeling run down, exhausted, and tired at the end of the day.

- Overcommitting Out of a Desire to Do Good- Many Empaths are do-gooders and want to help, support, nurture, and give care to other people. So often, the Empath will feel the need of another and go out of their way to help. This can become a way of life and eventually a way to hurt the Empaths overall health and well-being.

These problems and more can prevent an Empath from living more fully with their gift. If you have experienced some of these problems, you will be happy to know that they are easily remedied so that you can have a more fruitful and abundant experience. Moving forward into more of the hindrances to the

Empath's peace of mind, let's look at specific personality traits that can be particularly difficult for an Empath.

The Narcissist and the Empath

Narcissists and Empaths seem to be drawn to each other in general, and there is a reason for this. First, let's look at what each one really is: a narcissist is someone who lacks empathy and thrives on attention, acceptance, validation, and accolades; an Empath is highly intuitive, forgiving, compassionate, and willing to give everyone a chance, no matter what.

Because the narcissist is so hungry for praise and acknowledgment, the Empath is the perfect source of love because they will always be available to shower the narcissist with affection, forgiveness, and will often have an attitude of apology if they are doing anything that makes the narcissist unhappy or uncomfortable.

Unfortunately, this "attraction" can lead to life-long codependency between two unbalanced people: one is always thirsty for more of what's in the cup, and one's cup is always empty from filling the other's up. Not all relationships of this kind are romantic; sometimes they are professional, familial, or platonic friendships.

Either way, it is important as an Empath that you identify those in your life who may have these qualities or attitudes in your relationship together. Usually, an Empath will try to help or "fix" the narcissist, but loses themselves in the process, undermining their own personal growth and success to make another person feel wanted and needed all of the time. A narcissist can only help themselves heal by identifying the cause of their behavior, but will often prefer to latch onto others who will help them maintain their need to be adored all of the time.

Empaths struggle to let go of these kinds of relationships because of their desire to help others and to make them feel supported and loved. It is easy for a narcissist to charm an Empath at the beginning of a relationship because they are excellent at adapting to what others are like, manipulating their own characteristics to align more with the person they are choosing to be in a relationship with.

After a period of time, however, the narcissist will show all of their true colors and will demand that the Empath respond to their wishes, needs, and expectations accordingly. The humble and compassionate Empath will oblige in order to keep the peace and help the other person in their life feel good and happy, much to their detriment.

The lesson here is to create awareness about who in your life might be causing you more problems than you might have thought. Not all people are narcissists and not all narcissists latch onto Empaths. It is a common dynamic that can result in emotional pain and mental struggle for the Empath and so it is, therefore, important to know how to identify it in your current relationships or potential future ones.

What Are "Energy Vampires"?

Narcissists are one of several types of "energy vampires" as they are referred to, and all of them have the capacity to have a strong impact or influence on the Empath. Energy vampires are, by definition, someone who sucks or drains the energy out of you. To the Empath, they are a great cause of difficulty and concern because they can be difficult to avoid, especially when you are a person who has a desire to help, heal, or understand the perspective of others.

An energy vampire usually isn't aware that they may be difficult for the Empath to be around and have their own way of dealing with emotions and life matters. As someone who needs a lot of recharge and rejuvenation, Empaths will definitely experience needing to recharge after any interaction with an energy vampire. They have a tendency to take and not give anything in return. Sometimes, they can have very negative attitudes or behaviors that are the cause of distress for the Empath, or they can be overly connected to you because they need someone to listen to everything they have to say for as long as it takes to say it.

You may know a few of these people already in your life, and they could even be very close friends, family, or partners. One thing that can be a challenge for the Empath is boundaries with other people. Sometimes, Empaths are asking for this kind of energy outpouring from another simply by refusing to let someone know that they are not available to talk or that they won't allow someone to yell at them, in an effort to be compassionate and not hurt anyone's feelings.

The best way to handle these types of people is to offer them your time, friendship, or love in a kind way with healthy boundaries. If you know that someone is draining you of your energy, then you will have to learn how to express your needs in a kind and thoughtful way directly. This could mean having a reason to end the conversation you know will go on forever, or if someone is aggressive, you can share with them that you will prefer to talk to them once they have calmed down for a while. Later in this book, you will discover and learn more ways to help yourself create balance and boundaries with others in your life who seem to drain you of your energy.

There are a few common types of an energy vampire and they are:

- Narcissists- see the section above.

- Victim/Martyr- someone who can have an endless need for assistance or guidance but who also doesn't seem to want to find their own solutions to their problems. Along those same lines, a martyr may suggest that you are not seeing how hard they try to be of service, convincing you that they require praise for their suffering.

- Passive Aggressive- someone who is pleasant on the surface and then hits you where it hurts out of nowhere, especially if they are feeling unhappy, wounded, or emotionally frustrated about their life.

- Aggressive- someone easily inclined to be set off into a rage instead of appropriately dealing with their emotions. This can sometimes lead to physical violence or abuse and often causes anxiety in the people around this person.

- Dramatic- someone who craves drama as much as they like talking about it. Usually, a dramatic vampire is someone who will hunt you down to tell you the latest gossip and will continue on and on until the cows come home or until you give them a boundary.

Having awareness about the different kinds of people who can bleed you dry of your own energy is an important part of understanding your gift. Being an Empath can be very challenging, especially if you are not sure of how to handle certain personality types in the process. Energy vampires don't mean to be difficult or challenging, but as someone who absorbs energy and connects easily to other people's emotions, they can unknowingly cause you a lot of discomforts and emotional pain.

Downsides to Being a Powerful Empath

Like with any powerful gift or skill, there can sometimes be a downside. As you may have already guessed from your reading so far, being an Empath is not without its challenges and seeking to aid others because of your sensitivity to their needs can lead to a lot of problems in the long run.

Some of the major causes of an Empath's issues come from unwanted or unexpected energetic links to other people's thoughts and feelings. When you absorb the reality of another and make it your own, it can lead to a great deal of personal pain and suffering, especially when it is compounded over a long period of time and coming from several different people in general.

The problem of the Empath lies in their ability to work with their gift in a way that allows them to be a gifted person in the realms of caregiving, nurturing, healing, and loving all people without absorbing or taking on anyone else's life drama. Whether or not you feel like you are already good at this, it is important to stay in constant awareness of how other people's energy can greatly disempower you at any time, especially if you are not grounded or feeling balanced or well in your own life and energy.

Downsides to being an Empath only exist if you are not taking the proper measures to protect yourself, cleanse your energy of other's, and grounding within your power as an Empath and someone who has a capacity to give and receive energy powerfully. You can easily overcome these downsides with the proper use of healing tools, energy clearing, and meditation.

All of the downsides of this gift come from a lack of understanding about what you are, how it works, and what or who in your life is impacting you in a way that keeps you in challenging energy cycles or emotional down slides. The best way to identify for yourself what the downsides are for you is to consider the knowledge you have gained from these first two chapters and make a list of how you might be affected by other people's energy in your life at this time.

Ask yourself some of the following questions:

1. Do I feel supported by my partnerships?

2. Am I free to be myself around others in my life, or am I usually at the whim of other's needs?

3. Have I made sacrifices to make other people happy without making myself happy, too?

4. Are there people in my life who make me feel drained or exhausted every time I see them?

5. When I am in a relationship or partnership with someone? Do I let them have their way most of the time?

6. Do I get uncomfortable when other people ask me to talk about myself?

7. Are there workers in my office who make me feel sad, anxious, or low self-esteem, leading me to question my work skills and abilities?

8. Do I have, or have I had, a relationship that feels balanced and peaceful?

9. Are there members of my family or friend group that always make me feel worse rather than better?

10. What kinds of people in my life make me feel joy and acceptance, pleasure and comradery?

11. Do I surround myself with people that are grounded, balanced, happy, and honest with their feelings?

12. How many times do I tell myself that it is my fault and not theirs?

13. What kind of experience do I want to have with this person, and do I have it regularly?

14. When I am around a certain person in my life, do they like to listen to me talk about what's happening in my life or do they only talk about themselves first and foremost?

15. When I am around a certain person in my life, do they ask too much of me in regard to helping them with their problems, fate, or life circumstances?

16. If I let go of all of the feelings of other people in my life, how would I feel and what would that look like for me?

17. What are the kinds of people that I would like to be around in my life that make me feel supported and like I can be myself?

18. When I am around a certain person in my life, are they allowing me to have an opinion or telling me how I should think or feel?

19. Are their others in my friend group who feel the same way that I do about another person and are too polite to say anything about how they treat others?

20. Was my experience in my last partnership, friendship, etc. healthy and balanced, or challenging, difficult and emotionally toxic?

Make sure you ask these kinds of questions even as you are making new friendships or building new professional or romantic partnerships. The downsides to being an Empath come from how you choose to spend your life and whether or not you are ready to let go of the people, jobs, or places that cause you to feel stress and discomfort. Sometimes, it isn't even about letting go; it's about respecting yourself, creating healthy boundaries, and honoring your gift as an Empath.

There are so many wonderful benefits to having this experience or skill that outweigh the downsides and common problems. In the next chapter, you will learn so much more about the qualities of being an Empath and why it is such a powerful and important part of our cultural humanity.

Chapter 3: The Gift of Being an Empath

As you have read, there can be a lot of common problems and downsides to being an Empath, but there are equally as many wonderful attributes and life qualities that come from having such a powerful gift. It may not seem like it at first, but having an ability to sense and know how someone else is feeling on a deeper level can cause a lot of good things to happen, both for you and that person.

The act of empathy, in general, leads to a sense of wholeness and happiness; when we are good to others, we can be good to ourselves and we carry the positive vibration of love and harmony. Self-awareness of your own feelings and how you relate them to the world around you can be an excellent quality to demonstrate with all of the people in your life and can sometimes lead to a profession or career that utilizes your Empath skills for the betterment of many, not just a few friends and loved ones.

Seeing all of the ways that being an Empath can be challenging helps you to focus on how to bring the benefit of being an Empath into greater focus. In this chapter, you will learn more about how important this gift and ability can be in your home, personal, and professional life.

The Benefits of Being an Empath

Self-Awareness

Empaths are devoted to understanding how they feel and how others feel as a result of being so open to the emotional states of those around them and what is going on within. Many Empaths are highly self-aware due to the experience of needing to identify why, what, how, and when their sensitivities have an impact on their life and experience. A highly developed sense of self, or self-awareness, is an incredibly valuable tool for the path of all life and has a great benefit to the overall happiness and success of a person.

Seeing What Others Miss

Being highly intuitive and perceptive has its benefits and Empaths are naturally capable of witnessing, observing, and identifying what is happening all around them, almost like a detective at the scene of a crime. It has a lot to do with the Empaths understanding of what is happening under the surface and how people project that reality that the Empath is capable of "knowing." It can come in handy in a variety of life moments to have this strength of observation and perception.

Seeing Connections between All Things

Piggy-backing off of the previous benefit, being observant, and seeing more than meets the eye can allow an Empath to form underlying connections or links between people, places, circumstances, etc. It is the second component of being a good "detective" at the moment and can help someone move forward, or speak the truth of a situation with greater ease and understanding. Most of our daily lives are spent making connections like this in our brains and through our neural pathways. Because an Empath is naturally more observant and hyper-aware of unseen energy or forces of nature, they are therefore adept at making connections between all things.

Content with the Simple Life

Because life is a more intense experience for many Empaths, they can often be drawn to quiet, peaceful, simple lifestyles and are content just to be at peace or in a life circumstance that fits them well. Once you know you are an Empath and embrace the reality of how it feels to be so "in-tune" or "aware of all that is around," then you are likely to create a life experience that involves the simple pleasures and that can be of great benefit to your peace of mind, happiness of heart, and love of self.

Equally Subjective and Objective

Empaths are good at seeing all sides of a situation due to their ability to understand a scenario from both an objective and subjective reality. There can be disagreements and arguments, opinions and feelings, hard fact and theories, and the Empath is able to take open perspective about it all and form a uniquely balanced point of view through a desire to understand and not qualify or quantify unnecessarily. This can be a great gift in many life situations.

Creative Abilities

Empaths are often highly creative individuals. Because of their more sensitive natures, they are in a deeper connection and communication with their creative experience and have a tendency to with make works of art or to live a creative life that stands apart from what might be considered "normal." It usually follows that the Empath is one who "lives outside the box" because of their creative energy and their intention to find a healthy, energetic life balance for themselves.

Highly Sensitive to All People, Animals, and Places

Some might see this as a problem or a flaw. However, there is a great benefit to being sensitive to people, places, and animals. When you are hyper-aware of living things or environments, you can experience them more, and you can have a bigger, broader view of the whole world by "seeing" more of what is going on. Because Empaths can "know" what is going on through sensory perception, observation, and intuition, they are likely to see things coming before they happen. This can have a powerful use in life when an Empath is available to be this sensitive and observant. Another word to describe this sensitivity would be 'premonition.' In general, being highly sensitive to what is around you can offer you a wider scope of understanding, and therefore, a greater ability to experience success and progress. This usually only occurs if you are already energetically balanced, grounded, and understanding how to use your gift well.

Capable of Psychic Abilities

Allowing your energy to be open to other forces of nature can often align you with an ability to tap into your natural psychic tendencies. All people have the capacity to engage with this part of themselves, but more often than not, people are too afraid to know how to experience their psychic natures. Empaths, due to their overall gifts and tendencies, are far more likely to engage in these abilities because of their inherent capacity to sense and feel what isn't obvious or provable. Some psychic abilities that can surface for a well-balanced, healthy Empath are: clairvoyance, claircognizance, telepathy, visions or astral travel, speaking with "spirits," and more.

Healing and Helping Others

Empaths are natural healers. They want to help people, and this has a lot to do with how much they can sense and feel in another person without words or explanation. It can be of great benefit to our culture and society when Empaths follow their true calling and use their gift to help others heal. We are always looking for a general doctor or medical professional who makes us feel well-cared for and loved, through our need for healing and help. Many Empaths choose professions that help them offer health care or other healing services so that they can put their skills to good use. It is just as rewarding for the Empath to heal and help others as it is to the community they serve.

Sensitive to the Needs of Others

You have already read that it is a benefit to be highly sensitive to people, animals, and places. An extension of that high sensitivity is to be then able to determine what someone or something needs, based on what you perceive from their energy. Many people might call this intuition, and that is a good word to describe it; intuiting someone's needs is a hugely beneficial skill to carry through life and can be very valuable to all relationships. Before you get carried away telling your loved ones and partners that you know what they need, you might want to ask before you explain that you know better than they do, of course.

Quality of Life Enhanced

Intuitive and open, awakened and aware, the life of an Empath can have a heightened quality when you embrace your gift. When you are in alignment with the patterns and energies of how you are in this world, you stimulate all of the powerful ways to achieve your true purpose and live the life you want. As an Empath and being someone with these particular skills, they can be used to your advantage to help you improve your quality of life through focused determination to trust your gifts and skills. This comes in a variety of forms; however, it will always be linked to your concept of facing your path as an Empath and embracing your gift.

Everything is More Intense

Perhaps, this could be seen as a downside to being an Empath. However, life is not always as long as we want it to be, and there are many ways to appreciate and experience our journey. For an Empath, many things are a lot more intense on a daily basis, and this can actually be a benefit to your life as everything gets put into a much more enhanced perspective. There is a difference between being a drama king/queen and experiencing all of life's ups and downs, no matter how intense, with an open heart and open mind. Empaths can become very good at enjoying the intensity of their gift with the right mindset and balancing tools to see them through.

Excellent People Skills

Empaths are naturally gifted at dealing with people because of their sensitivities to their energy, emotions, needs, and underlying concerns. This is a benefit in many experiences, including love partnerships, when there is a healthy balance, friendships, parent/child relationships, workplace relationships, and even interactions with total strangers. Having a strong awareness of how other people's energy is affecting the energy all around you can help you determine the best way to approach a situation with a person and what is most needed at the moment. This, coupled with careful communication, can be one of the Empath's greatest skills.

As you can see, there are quite a few benefits to exploring and embracing your gift as an Empath. This list certainly doesn't cover everything, and you may discover even more benefits on your own unique path as you continue to develop your skills. Two of the biggest benefits that come into focus are Awareness and Healing/Helping Others. Let's look more deeply into the benefits and how they can help you achieve greater success as an Empath.

Self-Awareness and the Awareness of Others

Self-Awareness is a grand part of the life adventure of an individual. When we are looking within ourselves to find the answers we seek, we are developing our self-awareness. To many people, this seems like a given, but you would be surprised how many people look outside of themselves for answers. No one knows better than you, how to answer your life calling or how to move forward on your path.

A hyper-awareness of feelings, emotions, and energies are part of the life of an Empath, and so they are already more inclined to be self-aware as it is a part of how they learn to relate to the world around them. Some Empaths struggle with self-awareness regularly because they haven't learned how to balance or ground their energy, and then end up collecting other people's energy and emotions which can have a negative impact on their journey of self-awareness.

To find out more about how to work within the realms of self-awareness, all you have to do is connect to yourself. Ask yourself questions and keep on asking until you hit the answer you know is right because it has always been there inside of you. The capacity to draw upon your own self for information and knowledge is what helps you develop a stronger and more powerful self-awareness that leads to even greater expansion, growth, and personal transformation throughout the course of your life.

Empaths will always want to ask these questions because it is in their nature to look at these matters. As a result of connecting to their own self-awareness and process of being an individual, they are able to create and develop a deeper understanding of other people and how they might manifest their own realities and how it impacts their lives.

The benefit of this will always prove itself and as you learn to develop your own awareness of self. You will innately work on developing a sense and awareness of others. Often times, our egos can cloud our ability to receive a good sense of someone else and even ourselves and so it is a part of the lesson of self-awareness to leave your Ego at the door and bring with you only your intuition, energetic sensory perception, and a heart full of love, compassion, and empathy.

Here is a list of Self-Awareness Questions that can help you focus more on what is underneath your surface, just waiting to be answered:

1. How am I feeling right now?

2. Why am I feeling this way right now?

3. What happened just before I started feeling this way?

4. Has anything happened recently that made me feel this way?

5. Am I giving myself what I need today/ this week?

6. Am I allowing myself the things that I need in order to feel whole and balanced?

7. When was the last time I experienced joy?

8. What was that joy like?

9. Do I give enough space in my life for joyful moments?

10. When was the last time I felt vulnerable?

11. What caused me to feel vulnerable?

12. Do I avoid moments or experiences that make me feel vulnerable?

13. Are there people in my life right now that make me feel less like myself?

14. Are there people in my life right now that help me feel more like myself?

15. What are the ways that I control my energy or my emotions?

16. What are the ways that I deny my true self?

17. What does my true self like to do the most?

18. What does my true self like to do the least?

19. How long do I give myself to be quiet and relaxed without any obligation to anyone or anything, and is that enough time?

20. Where would I like to be in one year?

Take some time to answer these questions. Usually, your first instinct is the answer you are looking for. You can also create new questions that are more specific to your life circumstances and needs. Always ask yourself questions to develop your self-awareness. When you get better at knowing how to ask yourself these questions, then you will be a gifted Empath as you ask these questions of others.

Healing and Helping Others

One of the greatest instincts and inclinations of the Empath is to heal and help others. This can go two ways: well, or not good. There are plenty of good reasons to help others, and there are some times when the people you are trying to help on the emotional level do not want your help. This can be part of the problem for Empaths when they seek to help others because it is in their nature to do so, but it is not always wanted or well-received.

As you learn to hone in your special qualities and skills, you can use them for the advantage of helping people and also recognize through your senses and deeper understanding when the person you want to help is not welcoming your aid. The benefits of being able to help people so well because you can "see" what is going on under the surface is part of the experience of being an Empath. Looking for ways to help others is always a good path to travel, as long as you are awakened to the understanding that you cannot truly heal anyone.

Many Empaths lose sight of this on their journey, feeling empowered by their innate ability and gifts of understanding the feelings of others. When you lose sight of the true meaning of healing and helping others, you can cause more difficulty for yourself and the people you are trying to aid. An example of this might be offering advice to someone and realizing that they chose not to take it. You know that it would help them overcome something, but they are not interested in going on that journey. This can feel upsetting when you are certain it would be helpful for them. Empaths do well to remember that you cannot heal someone else for them; they have to choose it for themselves.

The gifts that come from being an Empath allow you to expose to others how well you can see a good path of healing and help; it doesn't always mean that the other person will take your advice or heed your knowing, but it can be a catalyst to a lot of growth for many people. The purpose of Empaths varies widely and many of them choose careers that allow them to aid people through their journeys of healing and wholeness because of their gifts and abilities.

When you begin to practice more of your true power as an Empath, you may find yourself drawn to a new career or profession that gives you the opportunity to help people heal themselves. There are many ways that these professions can manifest and in the next section, you will learn more about some of the commonly pursued professions of Empaths.

Possible Professions to Help You Thrive in Life as an Empath

There are a number of excellent choices of work if you are an Empath and some will not appear on this list since there are so many awesome ways to use your gift and skills. The following careers are some that are directly related to using your abilities to help others.

1. <u>Therapist/ Social Worker</u>- Therapy comes in a lot of different shapes and sizes and from a variety of perspectives and applications. Social work has a direct link to working in behavioral therapy and can be a very dynamic profession that deals with people and their progress. Either of these professions is heavily involved in the emotional experiences of others and how to help them find their way on the right path to creating the life circumstances that they want and need to thrive. Therapists are always discussing your feelings with you and are excited to aid you in your progress. Social workers help you to find a better way after trauma, neglect, and abuse so that you can live a healthier life. Some social workers even diagnose behavioral issues in their clients, and they are called Clinical Social Workers. An Empath would thrive in this career because of the need to understand the emotions of a person and help them facilitate change. What better role for someone who can deeply sense and feel another person's feelings? The one thing to be careful of for the Empath is that they maintain their own energy and are sure not to collect the energy of several clients back-to-back in a day.

2. <u>Healthcare Professional</u>- Whether you are a doctor, nurse, midwife, hospice worker, or naturopath, the work of the healthcare professional requires a great deal of compassion, understanding, and empathy. Most people have a need to seek medical care in the course of their lives and are looking for the healthcare professional who acts as a comfort to be near and someone who can truly respond to or understand the difficulty, pain, or even pleasurable life moment they are experiencing with their physical health. Empaths are excellent healthcare professionals because they are able to easily detect what needs attention and the best way to help each individual. There is always the term "bedside manner" that comes up when describing the quality of the healthcare provider you are working with. Empaths have a way of putting almost anyone at ease with their gifts of compassion and understanding and know what it feels like for their clients.

3. <u>Veterinarian</u>- It isn't always just about human beings; Empaths are gifted at understanding the feelings of animals and how to respond

well to them. An Empath would make an excellent Vet because of how well attuned they are to the energy of all living things. Some Veterinarian Empaths can even sometimes experience what feels like "hearing" or "sensing" what the animal or pet might be asking for or needing. This has been reported in several cases and is why some people choose to work in animal medicine in the first place: they just know what the animal wants or needs.

4. <u>Massage Therapist-</u> Massage is another form of therapy that involves the healing of muscles and tissues and may seem like it has nothing to do with emotions, but the body and mind are significantly linked. An Empath makes a good massage therapist because of how strongly they can feel what the person's body needs, how it has been injured, or where it needs the most work. Some Empath Massage Therapists have even reported occasionally hearing the worries or fears that can come up when they are working on someone in a therapeutic session. There are a lot of different massage modalities that are worth exploring if you are drawn to this kind of healing work and you can

offer couples' massage therapy with the next profession for an even bigger healing impact.

5. <u>Reiki Master</u>- You don't have to be a Reiki Master to perform Reiki therapy on someone, but it is the highest level you can get to in this specialized therapy that connects only to the energy centers and system of your body and does not involve any tissue manipulation, like a massage. Reiki is a unique form of healing therapy that derives itself from Eastern medicine and spiritual practices, especially those that correlate to chakras and auras. Your body's energy system is closely related to its physical qualities and health, and so when you are receiving an energetic healing experience from a Reiki professional, it is impacting not just your auras and your chakras, but also your organs, muscles, tissues, and even your thoughts and emotions. Paired with massage, this empathic healing work is a formidable force to help anyone align better with there personal health and well-being, outside of medical doctor visits. Empaths are already skilled at reading energy and so working as a Reiki professional is a good choice for them.

6. <u>Creative Artist</u>- Many Empaths are naturally creative because of how emotional art can be, either in the making or the appreciation of it. The act of creativity is a highly emotional process, and as Empaths are often very motivated by feelings and the energy of emotions, they are exceptionally good at making works of art. There are several different art forms and mediums like painting, drawing, sculpting, crafting, and so on that can help the Empath show off their true colors as a deeply sensitive and emotionally-giving being.

7. <u>Performance Artist</u>- Performing requires the ability to demonstrate a wide range of human emotion. Many actors and actresses can be Empaths because of their ability to understand and connect with human emotions on a deeper level. This is also considered a creative art and it uses fewer art supplies and is more about emotional expression through portraying a variety of characters and scenarios. Empaths do well in performance work because they can really feel who they are playing in a role. Other performance art can include different types of dance that allows the Empath to explore emotional expression through physicality. This

can actually be a very grounding profession for an Empath because it helps you stay balanced in your body while you explore emotions. Emotional expression can often take you out of your body and keep you living in your mind. Emotional expression through physical movement is a very empowering career opportunity for an Empath.

8. <u>Human Resources</u>- Many companies require a large number of people to keep them afloat and operating. Many employees need to be well-provided for and cared for in exchange for their hard work and dedication. Human Resources will usually act as a bridge between personal and company executives who need information about how to keep their employees happy. Without a human resource department, where would employees go to voice their needs and concerns about the job? Not every company works well with their employees in this way; however, the places that do have seen an increase in productivity in their employees because they feel more motivated to do a good job. Empaths make excellent Human Resource Managers because of their skills in helping people with their needs. Since Empaths can

sense the feelings of others, they can often use their gift to help many people at once and be a voice for the whole team, acting on behalf of the good of all the people on staff as well as people on the individual level when they have personal concerns and issues with their work.

9. <u>Child Care Services</u>- Empaths are very gifted in working with children who need a lot of presence, nurturing, and care. In today's age, so many mothers and fathers have to go to work every day and often need quality caregivers for their children while they are away from home. Empaths are adept at honoring the needs of most people, and usually, children need more emotional support because they are still growing and learning how to express their feelings. Empaths can be a great resource as childcare professionals because they can help a child better learn how to communicate their feelings and when they cannot, an Empath will offer them emotional support as needed. More and more children get put into daycare services every day and are away from their parents and so it is important that they are given tenderness, love, compassion, and understanding from

somewhere else. Empaths are excellent nannies, au pairs, and regular childcare professionals for these reasons.

10. <u>Humanitarian</u> – Many of the jobs already listed above may fall under the category of humanitarian work. There is a wide array of professions and careers that are considered humanitarian in nature. A humanitarian is basically someone who is concerned with or seeks to promote human welfare. Many Empaths are drawn to humanitarian professions because of how well they support the good of many. Other than the jobs listed above, such as healthcare professional, therapist, human resources specialist, and childcare services, some other humanitarian jobs include and are not limited to the following: education advisor, environmental engineer, communications specialist, grant and funding specialist, nutritionist, midwife, and birth assistant.

You don't have to be an Empath to choose these careers, nor do you have to choose any of them because you are an Empath. There are so many different kinds of jobs and careers that any Empath can find a way to thrive in. However, many of the careers listed above are some of the more common careers that Empaths are naturally drawn to because of their specific gifts and skills.

Empaths benefit from so many different parts of their energy and emotional experience and can find the right balance and grounding in their life to help them steer clear of the downsides and difficulties of being such an open and sensitive person. More often than not, with the right approach, tools, and energetic grounding, the benefits of being an Empath and the resulting quality of life greatly outweigh any of the problems and issues that can arise for you.

In the next chapter, you will learn even more about how to protect yourself from unwanted energy so that you can thrive in all you do and maintain healthy boundaries with the feelings and emotional experiences of others. You will discover methods for protecting yourself, the benefits of grounding your energy and what that means, and creative ways to keep yourself shielded from unwanted energy so that you can still participate in the life you want without losing any of your own personal power to someone else's feelings and energy.

Chapter 4: Healing and Balancing Tools for the Empath

Along your journey of self-discovery as an Empath, you may have already uncovered some of the issues that can limit your ability to live happily and fully with your gifts. In the previous chapters, you have read about so many of the common issues and problems that can arise for you if you are not working with your gift and awareness of how it works or how it can make you feel if you are not protected, prepared, and grounded for other people's energies.

You have read how these energetic imbalances can often manifest as physical sickness or illnesses, depression, anxiety, insomnia, and several other challenging emotional states. You have also read that when you are an Empath who takes good care of your energy and awareness of what is affecting you, then you can enjoy the benefits and gifts of being in-tune with people and your life overall.

Engaging in a healthy life practice to keep you emotionally, mentally, physically, and spiritually-supported is the best way to help yourself thrive as an Empath. There are a variety of ways to handle the unwanted energies of others and challenging situations; some of them you may already know or make space for in your life on occasion.

The purpose of this chapter is to teach you some of the ways you can take care of yourself in your daily life to make sure that you are accepting the truth of how you are so easily affected by the energy of others. Utilizing specific tools and energy clearing methods can make a huge difference in your life, especially if you are not using these methods in the first place.

As you begin to allow more time and energy spent on your own, working with your powerful gift, teaching yourself how to manage it and take care of it, you will begin to uncover the true meaning of your personal power and how it can give you more of the life that you want. Shielding and protecting yourself on a daily basis may be required, depending on how strong your Empathic skills are. Even if you have never done anything like that before, beginning to do it now will help you recover your truest self.

The following sections will go into more specific ways that you can utilize spiritual tools, the concept of energy clearing and how it works, the practice of mindfulness to keep your energy balanced and in awareness, and how meditation can be the ultimate balancing tool.

What Are Spiritual Healing Tools and How to Use Them

Spiritual tools come in many different shapes, sizes, and forms. They are simple to use and are always available to you when you need them. Some are objects, and other spiritual tools may be a calming practice or a meditation to help you realign with yourself. Anyone can reap the benefit of spiritual tools and Empaths are greatly impacted by the power of using them.

There are a lot of ways to look at how to use these tools and this book will offer a basic understanding and overview of what some of them are and simple instructions for how to bring them into your daily life practices. Over time, you may modify or create new ways of using these tools and will enjoy developing your own, unique relationship with them.

Crystals and Stones

People have been using the magic and power of crystals and stones for ages. They have become more popular in esoteric communities in our modern culture and are readily available at a variety of local shops and online retailers. They all have a strong, energetic property, and when combined with meditations and creative visualizations, they can be a very helpful way to rebalance, recharge, and refresh your energy.

They come in all different shapes and sizes, and each has its own unique property, quality, and characteristics that will benefit you. Crystals and stones connect directly to your energy field and provide you with a new way of energetically vibrating so that if you feel uncomfortable after a certain conversation or experience with a person, you can apply the energy of certain crystals to your body and will feel a shift back to your normal, energetic vibration.

Some people wear them as jewelry, while others carry them in their pockets or somewhere hidden on their person. You can also use them in a cleansing or rebalancing ritual at the end of a long day by laying them on top of your body, most commonly over your 7 chakras, to help you readjust and ground.

There are thousands of crystals that can be useful, and only you will know exactly which ones *feel* right for you. Trust your intuition to help you find the right one for your experience. Some examples of powerful energy clearing, grounding, or protection stones for Empaths are the following:

- Black Tourmaline – one of the most powerful protection crystals

- Hematite – protective stone; helps you find answers to higher questions

- Rose Quartz – can both open the heart chakra and also protect it from being too open to other people's unwanted energy

- Malachite – cleanse stagnant and unwanted energy

- Black Obsidian – protective of the aura energies; banishes unwanted energy

- Fluorite – helps you rebalance your emotions when they feel "off"

All of these stones are truly useful and beneficial to help you stay protected and shielded. At the same time, you may also want to engage with crystals and stones that can help you become more open and in-tune with your psychic qualities or ability to heal and help. Some of those crystals are:

- Amethyst – increases psychic capabilities; protection from any negativity

- Kyanite – heals and aligns all chakras and auras

- Lapis Lazuli – connects to greater energy, sometimes considered spiritual guides

- Quartz Crystal – helps keep your mind clear to hear the truth

- Labradorite – heightens intuition

You may not only want to protect your energy; you may also want to enhance it and empower it. These stones, together with the list of protective and shielding stones, can offer you a greater energetic balance in daily life. Find the crystals that resonate with you and get creative with how you enjoy them in your life.

Incense and Smoke

Many traditions today utilize incense and smoke for spiritual practices, but have you ever known the reason for it? The use of incense or smoke has occurred for centuries in ceremonies and rituals across cultures because of its ability to cleanse and clear space or the energy of the body. The aroma of incense can easily alter your state of mind or how you are feeling, so finding an incense aroma that is grounding and beneficial to you can be very useful to keep around the house when you need to "smudge out" unwanted energies.

Many people will use a bundle of dried sage leaves because of how cleansing its smoke and scent is. You may also find dried cedar, sweetgrass, and other herbal leaves that have a slow burn and produce a sweetly scented smoke that heals the energy of a room or a person. You can bring these types of spiritual healing tools into your daily life practices by simply burning them for their scent or by wafting the smoke through your home or around any area that feels energetically "stuck" or stagnant.

You can also waft the smoke around your body in order to clear and cleanse your own energy field. As an Empath, you may have to do this as often as every day, and as you become more comfortable with your gift, you may not need to do it as often or because you rely more upon other healing tools and practices.

If you are sensitive to smoke and scent, you may need to look for other healing tools that will benefit you more.

Salt and Water

Salt is an incredibly powerful grounding element and has the ability to shift energy back to its original state. Many people actually use warm salt water to cleanse their crystals and stones, which have an ability to absorb energy and hang onto it. Salt and water should be used on a majority of your crystals and stones in order to keep them in the balance as they work to keep you in balance. You only need to do this every so often, but it is helpful to know that in addition to using salt water on your crystals, you can use it on yourself to achieve the same results.

Water is a powerful cleansing agent. We bathe in it, wash our clothes and our dishes in it, and we drink it to stay hydrated and also to flush out the things inside of our bodies that we no longer need. Water can also perform as a cleansing tool to your overall energy and using it together with salt, can give you a powerful healing and cleansing experience.

You can have a hot salt water bath at the end of a long day and heal all of the collected and unwanted energy you may have connected to or collected. At the end of the bath, you can release that energy down the drain and consciously witness it depart, allowing a full energetic cleanse to take place.

Whether you are using it to clear the energy of your crystals and stones or whether you are using it to clear your body's energy, salt and water come together to perform a powerful clearing, grounding, and healing experience.

Sunshine and Earth

The power of the sun on your skin can almost always make you feel better. On a bright and sunny morning, going outside and letting sun rays glow on your face, as you close your eyes and take in the warmth of that yellow-orange light, can transform your energy. Additionally, the power of being outside in nature has a positive impact on your energy and is very grounding. Sitting down outside with some sun on your cheeks is a powerfully healing spiritual tool, and it costs you nothing but a little bit of your time.

Sunlight and Earth energy are an excellent tool for the Empath. Empaths need to spend time close to nature to recharge their batteries. We all could use a little more time outdoors and in nature, this is true, and once you recognize you are an Empath you may find that this kind of experience will feel different for you, especially if you are using your time to heal in nature and are truly enjoying its beauty from a healing and balancing perspective.

Not every day is bright and sunny, but you can still enjoy the powerful grounding quality of Earth energy as you look for tools to help you stay supported on your journey as an Empath.

By the Firelight

Like the warmth of the sun, the element of fire is a way for you to reconnect with your own inner fire and energy. Empaths spend a lot of time connecting to all of the other energy around them, especially when they find it difficult to stay balanced and grounded. Looking into the fire of a lit candle or having a fire in the fireplace or back yard fire pit can easily reconnect you with your own energy

Fire is cleansing and can also help you release and let go of unwanted energies, emotions, experiences, and feelings of your own, or other's that have been collected or felt.

Write down all of the things that you want to release from your energy on a piece of paper. Let the fire consume the paper, AND be very careful and take safety precautions when using fire as a healing tool. You can do this as often or as little as you like, but the act of physically writing your worries, feelings, or drama out on a sheet of paper and letting it burn up in the fire is an incredibly helpful way to release certain energies.

Meditations and Affirmations

The power of meditation is no secret; it has been utilized cross-culturally since the dawn of human beings' acceptance of spirituality. Meditation is simply an act of finding a quiet moment to connect to yourself through peaceful reflection. You may find a lot of rules, guidelines, or instructions online to teach the "right" way to do it, but there is no right or wrong way to meditate.

All you need is time, space, and a willingness to go deeper into yourself and listen. That's it! Meditation has an impact on your energy and how you are holding onto anything that you don't need. Many thoughts and emotions can arise while you close your eyes and go within; let them come up. The best way to understand what is really under your surface is to listen to your own thoughts and feelings and identify what needs to be released or cleansed.

Once you identify what needs release, you might find that affirmations can help you better let go of thoughts, ideas, and emotions that could be holding you back. Affirmations are simple and concise statements that help you achieve better self-awareness and personal growth, considering what you need to heal through meditation will show you how to create your affirmation.

Affirmations are positive statements that will help you identify your needs. Here are a few examples:

- I am willing to let go of that which does not belong to me.

- I am a powerful source of love, and I accept my sensitivity to other people's needs.

- I am thoughtfully exploring my decision to become awakened to my purpose as an Empath.

- I enjoy feeling and sensing things so strongly.

- I have the ability to enjoy this gift without letting go of who I truly am for other's needs.

Practicing meditation and affirmation will help you experience greater self-awareness and will also help you ground yourself and stay open and clear to your own energy as you explore and experience relationships with others.

Creative Visualization

Exploring your "inner eye" can add to your ability to see more clearly what others do not want to see. Creative visualization is another type of meditation and has an impact on your ability to connect to your own energy and spiritual journey.

The practice of visualizing is not as hard as some may think and only requires imagination and a desire to look at things with your eyes closed. After you get better at these skills, you will be able to visualize with your eyes open.

Close your eyes and picture an object in your mind. The object can be anything you want. Make sure to see its details: what color? Shape? Texture? Keep it in your mind and let it continue to develop detail until you can fully "see" it in your mind's eye. Practice this regularly and picture a variety of things. You may start to see landscapes, buildings, groups of people, animals, anything that comes up will have importance or meaning for you.

When you are better at using your creative visualization skills, you can use them to help protect you from unwanted energies. Sometimes, when you are in a conversation with someone, you may begin to feel drained by their energy. Bring your use of visualization into the situation and picture a shield of light around you. Make it a color that feels protective for you. You can also picture a sheer curtain between you, like a blanket that hangs between you and the other person's energy. This can help you feel shielded from their energy but still capable of engaging in the conversation.

Creative visualization has many applications, and as you explore your empathic gifts, you may find that it is useful in more ways than one.

Energy Clearing for the Self and Others

Now that you have a better understanding of spiritual healing tools and how to use them, you can learn more about the principles of energy clearing and what it really looks like. Many people have already begun to experience some of the concepts and ideas behind energy clearing and how it works from the practice of certain Eastern philosophies. Yoga has been an incredibly successful way for people to gain awareness of their bodies, breath, and energy since it arrived in the West several decades ago.

There are also other body and spiritual practices that delve more deeply into the concepts of our chakra system and why we need to keep it balanced. We all have energy, and it is organized throughout our body and the space surrounding it in a certain way.

Your body has 7 main chakras, starting at the base of your spine at the tailbone and going all the way to the crown of the head. These separate chakras each have a certain quality of energy, and when it is imbalanced, congested, or blocked, it can cause problems for your overall energetic balance. The chakras are directly linked to your ability to perform as a fully functional energetic life force, and they needed to be treated and healed just as much as your physical body may need attention or healing.

The root chakra is at the base of the spine. The second, or sacral chakra, is just below the belly button. The Solar plexus chakra is above the belly button and just below the ribs. The heart chakra is connected to the heart. The throat chakra is at the base of the neck. The brow chakra, or "third eye," is just above and between the eyebrows and the seventh, or crown chakra is at the crown of the head.

Each one of these chakras has a powerful impact on your physical, mental, and emotional existence. As these energy centers work to function normally, they can collect energies from other people, places, and things without your conscious knowledge of it. It is important as an Empath to have an understanding of the chakra system so that you can better understand how to clear and heal your own energy.

Your auras are all linked to the chakras in your system as well. Each chakra directly emits a layer of your auric field so that the root chakra's aura is closest to your skin and the crown chakra is furthest away from your body, sometimes, as much as two feet.

As you begin to understand these concepts, you can see how an Empath might easily acquire the energy of another. Being so open to anyone's energy as it extends 12-24 inches away from their body, no wonder you are able to pick up on their thoughts, feelings, and emotions. The best way to understand it is to first work on healing and understanding your own energy from this perspective and then learn how to continually rebalance, refresh, and ground the energy centers of your own body.

All of the tools mentioned in the last section can help with this process, especially when used regularly and in combination with each other. Over time, you will begin to see major results in your energy and how they function well. You will also have a better knowledge of when your energy is out of whack because you will have a keener understanding and awareness of how they function.

Energy blockages in the chakras are some of the most common reasons that people have personality disorders, mental and emotional health concerns, and even physical ailments like chronic headaches or fatigue, ulcers, and frequent colds or illnesses.

You cannot really clear the energy of someone else without their permission. However, if you are close to someone and you find that these methods work for you, you may be able to help them by showing them what you know about chakras and using energy clearing tools like the ones listed in the last section. You can always protect your energy. However, finding a method or routine that works best for you is a must. Your routine might change and evolve over time, and that's okay! Start with what feels good for you right now.

Some chakras may need more attention than others. Some will be less problematic in general over the course of your life, while others may always seem to need cleansing and clearing. The more you get to know your own energy, apart from other people's, the better you will be able to read into these senses and know how to help yourself release anything that is stuck or blocked.

Practice energy clearing with any of the tools that are listed in this chapter. You may also have some other tools that you know of that you can add into the mix. Be creative and have fun with it! Make your energy clearing routine as unique as you are.

Awareness and Mindfulness Practices

You have already learned in Chapter 3 about how self-awareness can be a benefit to being an Empath and some questions you can ask yourself to create more awareness. This is also a great way to create balance and healing for yourself. It is a benefit and a tool to help you stay in alignment with your energy and keep you grounded around others who may affect your energy.

Sometimes, in life, we have to face a lot of different challenges and situations; they just go with the territory of being human and living here on Earth with other people. Having a job, a home, a family, and friends, bills, and all of the other common possibilities of normal life can create all manner of interesting challenges and experiences, and part of the journey is valuing and appreciating all of these moments, even when they are difficult.

Empaths may have an even more uncomfortable or intense experience when they are dealing with these matters and have another level of sensing more than just what lies on the surface. Awareness is an excellent tool to keep you afloat in challenging times or during difficult relationships or conversations. When you step into a world of awareness, you can be better equipped to handle all of the energy involved so that it doesn't overwhelm you or discompose you.

Awareness leads to mindfulness and mindfulness is just another form of meditation. Working through life matters in a mindful way always helps you get where you need to go and when your energy is congested by others, creating awareness about it and mindfully returning to your internal balance can keep you grounded and safe in your experiences.

As with meditation, it requires an ability to see clearly and listen deeply. Unlike the principles of meditation, mindfulness can be practiced in the midst of any situation or moment. It requires that you pay very close attention to yourself (self-awareness) and to others or the environment so that you can mindfully approach it without letting it change your energy from what it wants to be to something else.

Mindfulness can be practiced and improved over time. It stems from the process of self-awareness and the careful observation of everything in the moment. Working with this as a tool to help you stay balanced and clear will give you a more empowered experience as an Empath.

Steps to a Grounding and Balancing Meditation

Now that you understand many of the tools that can be used to help you stay balanced and clear energetically, you can begin to give yourself more freedom to be yourself and have more healthy boundaries with other energies that you may be prone to collecting and experiencing.

The following steps to a grounding and balancing meditation will give you an idea of a simple method you can start using today to give you more energetic clearing and balancing. You can modify it as you see fit and incorporate whatever tools feel right for you. This meditation will include awareness, creative visualization, crystals, and smoke. You may decide that you would like to alter this meditation by performing it in a salty bath or lying outside in the grass in the warm sun. You can also perform this meditation in a quiet place in your home.

<u>*Grounding and Balancing Meditation*</u>:

1. Light your sage or other smudging stick and let it smoke for a moment. Wave it around your body and the place where you are going to lie down for the meditation. (You can snuff it out or allow it to burn during your meditation.)

2. Lie down on the floor, on a bed, or a couch so that you are in a comfortable position on your

back. Put a pillow under your knees if you need low back support.

3. Using one or more healing crystals and stones, place them on your heart chakra, third eye chakra and root chakra (for the root chakra stone, you can rest it on your pubic bone, or move it lower so that it is as close to your root as possible-on the upper thighs). If you only have one crystal, place it where it wants to be; use your intuition for the right placement.

4. Closing your eyes, inhale and exhale, relaxing into your body. Bring awareness to your body and sense where there is tension. Release any tension you may be holding onto in your body and fully relax into your whole body.

5. Notice the sounds of the room, the house, the street outside, but keep your eyes closed. Slowly shift your focus away from the outside world and bring it back into your body. Notice what the crystals feel like resting on your chakras. Notice any tingles, twitches, or feelings of vibration that might come up. Pay attention to your body's signals and let anything surface that needs to.

6. Keeping your eyes closed, begin to visualize the chakras in your body. See their energy and how it is moving, or not moving, within you. Let any images come up that want to. You may start to see things that you don't intend to picture, but that is just showing up.

7. As you continue to breathe and relax your body, visualize your hand moving toward any chakra that seems congested or blocked. With your imagined hand, pick up any pieces of energy or shadowy objects that seem like they are blocking your chakra. See your self pulling it away from your body and throwing it away from you. You can repeat this with any chakra that seems like it needs attention.

8. Now, visualize all of your chakras again and see how they are moving and feeling. Do they look more open, more active? Are they more colorful? Do you feel a new sensation in your energy?

9. Continue to breathe deeply and relax your body for a while.

10. When you are ready, sit up and re-light your incense or smudge stick and cleanse the air around you, fully releasing and letting go of any energy you "pulled" out of your system. You are now grounded and cleansed.

This meditation is a simple version of something that you can build upon. It will be unique to you, and the more you practice it, the better you will become at grounding and cleansing. Each time you do, it will be a completely different experience, depending on what needs grounding and clearing. Some people find it helpful to keep a journal or a log of their meditation practices so that they can better process the emotions, thoughts, and visuals that can come up when you are doing this kind of meditation.

Experiment and explore, and you will find a new way to embrace your life as an Empath!

Chapter 5: How to Keep Unwanted Energy from Influencing You as an Empath

Welcome to a new layer of understanding your gift. The journey so far has shown you a great deal about what it means to be an Empath, some of the common problems and downsides to having this gift, the glorious benefits that can result in your healthy participation with your skills and abilities, and what kinds of healing tools may be useful in keeping you energetically grounded and clear.

This chapter will offer some more practical examples of how you can keep unwanted energies from influencing you. It might be new to you, or you may already have an understanding of how to apply these tools; either way, learning how to enjoy your life experience as an Empath without letting other energies influence you will be of great importance on your journey.

As you begin to practice the methods from the last chapter to help yourself stay clear and grounded, you now need to be able to prepare for what happens out in the world when you are encountering all of the energies you want to protect yourself from. Starting off on a grounded foot is a great way to begin.

Preparing for your day with a grounding meditation can keep your energy true to you and vibrate on high levels, making it that much harder to discompose your energy when you have certain encounters.

Nevertheless, there are always those intense moments or people who can rearrange your energy and cause you to question or doubt how you think or feel at the moment. Practicing using these tools and methods at the moment can be very useful and you should work with them in whatever way is possible for you in those moments.

When Other People Are Negative: Ways to Protect Yourself

Negativity is all around us every day. People wear their hearts on their sleeves and carry their worries on their shoulders. We are all struggling with something at some point in our lives, and when we feel burdened by it, it can be very energetically obvious. Many people don't even realize how negative they are being because it is how they live through a majority of their day, unable to move past whatever emotional pain or drama is keeping them in that cycle of thought and emotion.

Empaths are especially sensitive to the negative people in their lives and even more susceptible to collecting the negativity exuded by these individuals. They aren't bad people nor do they deserve to be shunned for the quality of their energy; often times, they are just going through a challenging part of their life journey, and all you can do is have compassion for them.

As a matter of necessity, an Empath will need to protect themselves from unwanted negativity, even from close friends, family, and loved ones and this can be challenging, especially if you want to help them feel better. Before you make any attempt to make a negative person feel better, you need to protect yourself. You can use crystals and stones that you carry with you, or you can perform affirmations or simple meditations to ground you before engaging in conversation with this person.

It helps to create awareness about it beforehand. By acknowledging that the other person is in a negative mood, you are already protecting yourself from their energy, knowing that you can still be a friend, but that you will not need to carry away their burden with you.

Not all encounters with negative people are with whom you care about and love. Sometimes, you may have a coworker or a boss who always seems to be in a sour mood, and you have no choice but to be near them because of your professional relationship. Having to be around someone with that attitude every day can feel awful to anyone, especially Empaths.

When you are at the office, you can keep yourself grounded by using some of your affirmation, mindfulness, awareness, and meditation tools in order to prepare you for encounters that you know are going to happen, like if you have to attend a meeting or a consultation with this person involved.

You may be caught off guard by an encounter with them and feel yourself getting weaker or more drained by their energy at the moment; this would be an excellent time to practice mindfulness and self-awareness. You can even repeat an affirmation in your mind that you use to stay grounded. You can even create an affirmation specifically for this person in order to help you feel capable of conducting business with them without being affected by their negativity. (Ex: I know Bill is under pressure and his pressure doesn't belong to me. I am able to explain my needs to Bill without worry about how he will react because he always reacts and that's not my fault or my concern.)

Keeping crystals around the workplace might feel awkward for some people, but you can keep one in your pocket and hold onto it when this person approaches you, or you can wear it as jewelry, like a ring, bracelet, or necklace.

Another method to try is through working with creative visuals to help you stay shielded from the negative energy. You may know that this person is just going through a hard time and you want to be understanding, but that doesn't mean you can't protect yourself from their emotional energy. Imagine that there is a thin fountain of water, like a waterfall or curtain of water flowing between your bodies. You can still see them through the water and hear them, but there is a powerful element there to absorb and wash away any of their negative energies before they can reach you.

It may take extra practice to get good at these kinds of visualizations, but it has a powerful way of protecting you. You could also perceive an animal guardian who stands or sits in front of you, who will take all of the negative energy into them for you and be your protector. See a lion or a bear. You could also see your beloved dog, or even a giant dragon if you want. There are no limits to the imagination except for the ones we put on it. Get creative with imagining what your guardian animal would look like and have them come with you into the conference room.

As you begin to practice energy protection using the tools from the previous chapter, you can start to work with them in practical ways. One of the best ways to practice using these tools is in these circumstances when other people's negative energy or emotions seem to fill the whole room. Always have compassion and understanding while you balance, ground, and protect yourself. Most people aren't even aware that an Empath is standing right in front of them and feeling how bad they feel. That is why learning to protect yourself from energy is so important and can even be creative and fun.

Grounding: Before and After

You already learned about how to ground and why; so, *when* do you ground yourself? Every Empath is different, and at different skill levels on their unique journey, so it is hard to say what will be best for any individual's experience of when to do something. In general, a good rule of thumb for an Empath who has a high sensitivity to other people's energies, grounding *before* and *after* an experience or encounter can be the best way of maintaining a good balance for yourself.

It certainly will depend on the quality of the experience you are having or the type of person you are in front of. You may not need to ground before or after every time. However, you will always be a little bit susceptible to engaging with and connecting to someone's energy field. If you are new at exploring your gifts and are just learning the best ways to handle unwanted energy, make time and space for grounding yourself before you walk into a situation, especially if you already know it will be a difficult or challenging experience.

You may have a friend that you are close to who has a lot of drama in their life. Every time you hang out with them, you feel drained afterward because of how strong their energy can be for you. Preparing yourself ahead of time might make it an easier experience for you and you can also carry your protective crystals with you to give you some extra grounding and shielding. Your friend doesn't even need to know that you are holding a protection stone with you: it isn't about their energy; it's about yours.

It may be helpful, as you depart from your time together, to create a moment to ground yourself by creating self-awareness around your energy. Tap into it and see how you are feeling. Ask yourself if there is anything you need to do to clear your energy after hanging out with your friend. It can be as simple as stating affirmations in your car or driving to the nearby park to relax in the grass and ground yourself with Earth energy. Whatever way you like to ground, you can carry it with you and use it as needed while you go through your day and explore and experience your relationships.

Taking time to ground yourself daily is also helpful. Instead of grounding before and after a situation or encounter, see it as grounding before the day begins and after it ends. Incorporate some of the techniques and tools you have learned into your morning routine so that you can start your day balanced, energized, protected, and grounded. At the end of the day, after several situations and encounters, you can perform another routine to help you realign with your energy. Take a hot salt bath and meditate to get you back to your normal energy levels or sit in your back yard with a cup of tea or water and mindfully enjoy the end of the day as it turns into night.

You have the creative power to decide how to ground. Choosing when to ground is up to you and the more often you do it, the better you will feel. Try the Before and After rule to help you create some stability and balance in your everyday life.

Communicating Boundaries

This may seem obvious; however, for a lot of Empaths, being honest and straightforward about your needs may be a challenge out of a desire to make other people feel happy and welcome. You may have had challenges creating boundaries in your relationships in the past, and because of this, it has had a negative influence on your energy. The toughest part of stating a boundary is feeling the other person's reaction to it, and for an Empath, this is what you want to avoid: causing discomfort in others so that you don't have to *feel* it.

Empaths have to learn how to communicate their own needs in order to work with their gift in a healthy manner, in order to keep unwanted energy from influencing them. So, how do you create boundaries with people in your life, especially when you have already shown them that you have so few?

The answer to that is unique to you and your situation, but here you can learn some simple guidelines to follow to help you with clear and truthful communication which will allow you to offer the boundaries you need to share with others in your life.

<u>Clearly Communicating Boundaries: Simple Rules and Guidelines:</u>

1. **Be direct.** Open up to whomever you are talking to with honest and clear-cut language.

    Ex: I am okay with you being late sometimes, and I am not okay with you being late every time.

2. **Use feeling words to express yourself.** Using the phrase "I feel" when you are talking to someone allows them to understand that you have emotions involved in your experience that need to be valued and respected.

Ex: I feel uncomfortable around you because you don't listen to anything I say and cut me off when I am talking. I feel sad that you don't want to hear what I have to say.

3. **Be willing to accommodate compromise**. Sometimes, when you are clearly communicating with a person and open up about your needs, they begin to share their previously uncommunicated needs. This can lead to a conversation between you to help you arrive at a clearer way of spending time together.

Ex:
Person A: When you don't respect my time, it makes me feel rejected by you.

Person B: You always seem like you aren't interested in spending time with me and I feel rejected by you.

Person A: I will make it clearer when I am able to spend time with you and communicate with you when I can't.

Person B: I will be more aware of your personal time and that you may need to be alone more often.

4. **Be honest**. You may be inclined to protect someone else's feelings at the expense of your energy and feelings. Over time, this can have a detrimental impact on your energy. Choose declarative statements that are an honest representation of how you are and what needs to happen in the situation.

    Ex: I am tired and hungry and this isn't a good time for me to talk.

5. **Express interest in a person's point of view without making it your own.** Empaths are highly agreeable, even when they don't agree, and this can cause problems later, especially when they need to create a boundary with a person. Allowing others to have a point of view while still maintaining your own is a good way to set a boundary with them.

Ex:

Person A: Well, I think we should go to this party and see if we can get some extra fun tonight.

Person B: I agree we should get some extra fun tonight; however, I am feeling a need to go home and rest and want to find the fun at home.

Boundaries are essential to an Empath and no boundary can be effectively created without proper communication. The art of communication is a skill all people ought to know and practice, and in the case of being an Empath, it can make a huge difference in how you spend your time and energy. Good boundaries, even with those closest to us in our lives, are the way to ensure that you maintain a healthy relationship with yourself, your energy, and other people and theirs.

You can use boundary communication as a tool to assist you in the management of your own energy and the ability to steer clear of the unwanted energy of others. You may have to face some awkward moments and tell people what they don't want to hear, but it will help you exercise your right to have an open relationship with your gift as an Empath and your right to empower yourself as a person with a choice. You can choose to release yourself from uncomfortable situations with other people by using clear communication and establishing effective and mindful boundaries.

All of the concepts and techniques in this chapter are a guideline and tool to help equip you in situations when you feel like you are being subjected to unwanted energy. Use them as needed and practice them often. You don't have to be an Empath to find these tools useful, but for the Empath, they are an excellent way to help you keep yourself grounded, shielded, and empowered within your own energy.

Chapter 6: Quality Space and Time

Energy is the crux of all sensitivities and issues that can arise for the Empath. There is low energy and high energy, or positive and negative vibrations. Empaths who don't understand this concept will find it difficult to correlate why they feel a certain way when they would like to feel another. When you examine the concepts behind how your energy works and how, as humans, we are always in a constant exchange with the energy of all things around us, you can begin to understand a deeper and broader view of how people function in the world and what causes our personal dramas and joys.

Energetic reading, or sensing, is how the Empath experiences the world around them. All people do this on some level, but for the Empath, it is a visceral and daily experience that cannot be ignored. Perceptions of how other people's energy might be influencing their lives are one of the ways an Empath can have openness with what other people are going through, and it can also be very energetically consuming.

As you have read in the previous chapters, there are several ways that you can protect, shield, ground, and cleanse your energy so that you can feel your own wants, needs, emotions, and personal energy more fully. The tools you have read about are several ways to handle a daily barrage of unwanted energy from people or situations that cannot be avoided because of your need to work and live in the world.

For many, a need for solitude or space from others has its own way of shielding, protecting, and rejuvenating. For the Empath, this is often a vital and necessary component of life, and many Empaths seeks quiet alone time and space from their friends, loved ones, and colleagues in order to feel refreshed.

On this path to understanding your gifts and skills, you may want to realize some of the ways that you give yourself this time and space to reflect and replenish. Are you getting the time you need to refill your energy? Are you able to have a safe place or sanctuary in your home to collect your thoughts and be alone? Do you feel overwhelmed and exhausted by too many social activities and plans? Are your relationships uncomfortable at times because you never get to do anything by yourself?

Many relationship dynamics are a challenge for Empaths because of their need for space and time. There are lessons to learn in all relationships and when working with your abilities to sense other people's feelings, you will have to learn more about how some relationships may need less of your time than you think. Where do you feel the best in your relationships? Are they giving you what you want and need, or deserve? Are there people in your life who are always making you feel differently than you want to feel?

These questions are worth asking if you are an Empath. In this chapter, you will learn more about the reality of why you will need more time alone than other people might. You will see how the quality of space and time you offer yourself can have a hugely beneficial impact on your general well-being and state of mind. You will also discover what it can be like for your relationships and how to discover the healthiest ways for you to enjoy compatible and balanced partnerships while you explore and honor your empathic abilities.

Why You Should Limit Time with Other People or Groups

While you have read through these pages, have you noticed a common theme? Empaths need space from another person's energy. Whether it is through the use of tools to banish or clear unwanted energy that feels "collected" from your time together, or whether it is creating boundaries about how you can spend time with someone, these are all methods to help the Empath create space with the energy that they receive from other people, groups, and places.

There is a significant change in feeling when an Empath walks into a room of people who just had a big argument. Many people could walk into the same room and feel like something is "off," while others wouldn't perceive anything at all. To an Empath, the room is thick with discomfort and potent negative energy. Realizing how your energy is so easily affected by the unwanted energy of others, you will want to give yourself enough time and space from other people so that you can experience your own grounded, clear, and balanced energy more regularly.

As you improve your skills of protection and grounding, you can better prepare yourself for those challenging moments when you walk in on the discomfort that other people left behind in a room, but you won't always be able to protect yourself fully. Some energy is so strong and uncomfortable, it will have its way with your sensitivities and you will have to ground yourself after.

Many Empaths struggle to keep a healthy balance as they get more open to their reality and what causes their feelings and emotions to shift while they are around a person, a group, or even an environment or space. The question is: what can you do to help yourself stay more positive in your energy?

Limiting time and space with others might seem like a tragic life choice. After all, we all need people and want to have love and support from our community and relationships and we all need to be able to make connections with all of the people in our lives, no matter how intense their energy may feel to you. On the other hand, Empaths find a lot of pleasure and peace in quiet time and space to be alone. The reason for this is because they are able to have more control over the energy they are feeling and the quality of energy in the environment or space they are in.

Take the workplace, for example, you sit in an office at a desk under fluorescent lights for 8 hours 5 days a week, looking at a computer screen and taking phone calls. The energy of the building is a challenge for you because of the lighting, the activities you have to work on, and also the entire office full of people's energy. All day long, you are working hard to shield and protect yourself from the quality of energy you are working in; you have to have a job, right?

At the end of the day, a few of your coworkers invite you out for drinks and appetizers, wanting to continue the time together to bond over the work day or talk about the boss. For you, that is the last thing you want to do. Empaths are significantly more likely to go to where they can recharge their batteries after being out of their energetic comfort zone for so long. Finding sanctuary is better than any post-work cocktail at the local bar for the Empath. That is not to say that Empaths aren't game for a good time; they are! But in this case, after hours of the workday spent absorbing energy with a group of people in an office, you might be most interested in resting and recovering your energy.

More often than not, an Empath is considered an introvert. Introversion is a personality trait that describes how someone is inclined to go within and focus on internal thoughts, feelings, etc. The opposite of that is Extroversion; people who seek outside stimuli and spend less quality time in reflective moods or periods. Introverts need quiet and solitude to recharge their batteries; extroverts need stimulation, activity, groups, and human contact. The world is full of both and you can certainly be an extroverted Empath.

However, Empaths tend toward introversion, and as such, look for more opportunities to find the right place and people at the right moment so that they can feel a balance with their need to be on their own and reflect more frequently than extroverts do.

Let's take another example: In your house, you share space with another roommate who has a lot of intense and dramatic energy. You care about your roommate and enjoy their company, in general, but you find yourself needing to close off in your own part of the house frequently so that you can conserve your energy. Your roommate has a lot of people come over to hang out, even when you are hoping for more serenity and peace. You know that you have to share the space together and that it isn't fair for you to ask that your roommate limit the number of guests that come over or the frequency of parties or get-togethers.

You also need to share the space and make it clear that you are in need of more peaceful time to enjoy relaxation and that you need to have a balanced compromise in order to remain roommates. Your roommate may not understand why you are so particular about wanting to have a schedule or a house rule about parties and guests, but you will need to offer a boundary of how you want to share the space, even if it means that you have to explain that you are sensitive to loud noises and people's energy and that it is hard for you to have so many guests over several times a week.

Empaths need space and time in which they don't have to worry or think about other energies. People are also a very stimulating experience to an Empath, so even if you decided to join the party your roommate is throwing with a few guests, you may only be able to sit comfortably with everyone for a period of time before needing to retreat into your own space. This kind of feeling and behavior is not uncommon for Empaths and you will know this to be true if you are one yourself.

Time and space are needed in order for you to feel rested and replenished, and it is always okay to ask for these things or to give it to yourself. Time and time again, you will find that as you expand your knowledge about your true nature and how it actually feels to live as an Empath, you will recognize the value and virtue of spending time on your own and in a space that feels right for you.

Spaces are another impactful energy overall and can carry or hold onto a lot of feelings. Empaths notice after someone leaves a room that their energy was sad or depressed. Empaths can also tell when they walk into someone's home for a dinner party that the couple who invited them over for dinner just had a fight but are acting like they are perfectly fine. Energy hangs in the air and it is easily picked up on by an Empath, like a detective solving a mystery, based on their senses alone.

If you live in your own home or apartment by yourself, then you have a good handle on the quality of energy in your space and know how to maintain it the way you like. Let's say you invite a friend over that you haven't seen in a while and you have some catching up to do. Your friend has a lot of drama to talk about and does most of the talking while you listen. After your friend leaves, you feel that the energy of your living room has altered and feels heavier. The energy of your space is significantly different because of your friend's energy. Now would be a good time to get out your incense or smudge stick and clear the energy of the room.

Empaths will discover this as they move through life and as you bring more awareness to honing in on your skills of detecting energy, you will be better able to notice when things have shifted and felt "off" so that you can realign them. Some places you won't be able to clear or balance the energy in nor can you always do this with the people that you encounter, but you can change your own energy by grounding and clearing. Giving yourself appropriate amounts of space, and time and limiting your time with people, are an essential tool for the Empath.

Limiting your time with others is not a bad thing, especially if you need space to reflect and rejuvenate. Much of your quality alone time is a way for you to connect more with your own energy and your self-awareness. It is a vital experience for any person to create time and space for these reflective moments, and for the Empath, they are what makes for a healthy and balanced life.

Space and Time for Reflection and Rejuvenation

Empaths need plenty of time alone, as you read in the last section. You need it so that you can better protect your energy from the unwanted energy of others and to ground and balance your whole self in order to thrive and experience the life that feels best for you. Offering yourself quality space and time to reflect is an essential need for Empaths and the rejuvenation and replenishment that comes from these times will benefit you greatly.

Connection to your own energy is the best way for you to create harmony in your life and with so many other energies around you, it may not always be easy or possible. That is why you have to create the space and time for it on a regular basis and when you do, it will need to be time for you to rest and replenish your energy.

Empaths are looking for solace from the unwanted energies that linger all around them or connect to them for longer periods of time that are needed or wanted. Special allowances can be made, of course, for Empaths who choose to work in professional fields where they are working to help other people with their needs, but all Empaths will benefit from some well-deserved reflection and rejuvenation time.

There is no medical doctor in America who will diagnose you as being an Empath and prescribe rest and relaxation to you. Any therapist you see will likely understand the possible cause of your energetic exhaustion and might point out to you that you are an

Empath, but they may not have an understanding of what tools you can use to ground yourself or what benefits you the most on your path.

Considering the amount of time we all have to spend at our jobs and out in the world running errands and taking care of the business of life, it stands to reason that we would afford ourselves equal quantities of time to reflect and rejuvenate. Sadly, this is often not the case. Our culture is less composed of participating in personal wellness and more concerned about achievement, wealth, and ownership. The possibility of declaring and executing specific times for reflection and replenishment are less likely to occur in a society that has such demands and so anyone in awareness of their need for it must create an opportunity for it.

The best way for an Empath to connect to their own needs and energy is to plan and schedule these times for peace and recovery. It may seem silly to you if you haven't considered it before, or if you haven't acknowledged your empathic skills until now, however, the planning and scheduling of space and time for reflection and rejuvenation are what will promote your healthiest and most meaningful life.

Now, knowing about how challenging and difficult it is to be an Empath when you are not taking care of your energy, you can see how valuable and important it truly is to spend time on your own and to offer yourself quality time to truly rest and recover your energy. The possibilities are endless for how you can practice spending this time and the following list is an example of ways that an Empath might take pleasure in planning reflection and rejuvenation time.

- Quiet meditation- finding a quiet place where you will not be disturbed, devoting an hour or more to reflecting through the practice of meditation.

- Setting Hours- determining hours in the morning or at night when you will not answer emails or phone calls

- Spa Day- if you don't want to go to a spa that will be crowded with other people, you can treat yourself to a spa day at home with special products you enjoy and plenty of time to feel luxurious and relaxed.

- Nature walk- spending time in nature is good for the soul. It offers time to quietly reflect and connects you to the energy of Earth which naturally rejuvenates your energy.

- Receiving Reiki, Acupuncture, Massage, or other body treatments- taking the time to schedule relaxing and healing services is an excellent way to refresh and rebalance your energy. The soothing physical contact is also important to an Empath, who may have a need to limit some of their time with other people. Being with a healing therapist who offers their services to you through a variety of formats is a calm, peaceful, and gentle experience to help you align more fully with your clear and cleansed energy.

- Spending time in your apartment or home without technology- surprisingly, this is really hard for people, but the internet and excessive use of technology can have a major impact on your overall energy. At the time, it may feel like a good thing, to scroll through social media and gaze at everyone's life. For the Empath, you are scrolling through a lot of energy that you don't need to pick up and carry around with you. Taking time away from technology can have a huge benefit, especially in times that you need to relax and rejuvenate. Give yourself a few hours of no cell phone and no internet and just "be."

- Schedule a quick trip or getaway to a remote place- finding places that make you feel grounded and whole are places you can visit to create time and space for reflection. You may prefer the mountains or the desert; you may know of a great campground or quiet spa retreat that you can visit. Setting aside space and time in your calendar to go to the places that help you focus on your need to replenish and restore your energy will give more meaning to the experience and more respect to your need to have these times to yourself. You may enjoy it with a partner, or you may prefer it alone, but either way, spending time on a holiday geared towards reflection is a perfect way to refresh yourself.

- Attend a workshop or retreat for meditation- Going to a meditation retreat can bring you into deeper contact with your needs and your desires. Many of the people who attend these retreats are looking for a calm and reflective experience as well, and so you wouldn't need to be concerned about sharing the experience with others. Having some community during your period of quiet reflection can feel very supportive and energetically pure and light. Many retreats offer accommodations and can help you get into closer connection with your higher self and work as an Empath.

This list is a way to get you started as you come up with creative ways to give yourself space and time. You may like all or none of these possibilities and it is up to you to find the way that you like to spend time in your own world of energy with your own reflective thoughts and experiences. Journaling at these times can be highly beneficial because as you reflect and make room for opening and awakening within yourself, you may need to put a lot of it down on paper as a way of releasing those thoughts, ideas, and memories from your energy.

Play around with how you like to spend your time relaxing and refreshing yourself. Try to open up your world of empathy with ideas that resonate most deeply with your true wants and desires. Be accepting that you need to enjoy these times peacefully and without disturbance from others and have fun with it! You deserve to enjoy space and time for reflection and rejuvenation.

Relationships and the Empath

One of the most important realities for any person is the relationships they have with someone or a group. People need people, and we are all looking for love, companionship, connection, and camaraderie. The life of an Empath is one of great sensitivity and energetic openness and requires a lot of protection and grounding, but that doesn't mean that you cannot thrive or have incredibly healthy and nurturing relationships.

Several people might be warned against certain kinds of relationships or people because of how toxic or challenging they are. For an Empath, that can be true of any relationship if you are not properly guarding and replenishing your energy. Often, Empaths will get involved with people who are needy and attention seeking and who want a partner who can fulfill their inner needs more. For any person, it is impossible to offer them what they cannot truly give to themselves in the form of self-love, and for an empath, it is true that they will work tirelessly to help someone feel truly desired and loved, even when that person doesn't feel that way about themselves.

Personal partnerships are incredible places for you to learn more about the qualities of your gift and how to strengthen it. All of our relationships help us grow and achieve a deeper sense of self and personal knowing. Empaths work hard to help and heal others, and so it can be a challenge to find the right balance of love and boundary.

Here are some common issues that can arise for an Empath in a romantic relationship:

- *Codependency-* usually, the Empath is the partner providing the most support to the other person, leading to a significant imbalance and an excessive emotional and psychological dependence on the Empath. This can be very toxic energetically for you and can leave you feeling drained and burned out without really understanding why. Common elements can include codependency when a partner has an addiction to something or has an affliction or an illness that requires additional care from someone. A narcissist and an empath will often engage in codependent behaviors as well.

- *Relinquishing Control-* Empaths are always working towards peace and harmony, and so in many partnerships, they can be the "doormat" so the other person can have their way and make all of the important decisions, even when they may not be a good choice, just to keep the peace.

- *Loss of the Self*- Empaths want to help their partner feel special and important and to have all the success they want and deserve. Empaths will work tirelessly to support the dreams and passions of their partner at the expense of their own, losing their own purpose and truth in the mix. This can create very low energy in a person and it may be that, as an Empath, you start to feel like you deserve to be less than the one you love.

These can be very easy situations to fall into, and they never really feel like this when you are first falling in love with someone. Over time, as you bond and connect more, these types of relationship dynamics can start to show up, and it is up to you and your partner to respond to them and determine a solution.

Romance is a huge part of being human, and as an Empath, you are always drawn to certain types of energy that feel good to you. When they feel off or bad and make you uncomfortable, then you are not as likely to commit yourself to that person. When you meet someone and the sparks fly, you get a chance to feel the energy of love and connection that helps you to feel strong compatibility with another and you work to maintain that feeling for as long as you can.

Slowly, over time, things shift; people grow and change, or you start to see their true colors once they are comfortable enough to show them. We all have something we don't want to show off on the first, second or even 100th date with someone, but it is always there and cannot be hidden from an Empath. You will always feel if something is a little off or skewed, and when you work with your partner to determine the energetic cause, they may grow defensive and distant.

Empaths can have a challenging time in relationships because of these factors. Being able to "see" and sense someone else's energy can be a hard experience for you because your partner may not want to open up to you about what they are vulnerable about. Since you can feel and sense their vulnerability or any other emotion all of the time, all you will want to do is expose it and resolve it. This leads to an epic back and forth between the Empath and their partner as they romantically butt heads about how to resolve personal growth.

What you can learn as an Empath in your romantic partnerships is how to process your own feelings with yourself and protect and shield your own energy so that you are capable of handling these moments, remaining grounded and secure in your own energy without taking on the emotional state of your partner. You can still be loving and compassionate with someone without actually "feeling" their pain, but for the Empat, it is a real challenge and requires personal effort and discipline.

Love bonds are strong, and if you are discovering through reading this book that you are an Empath, you may be questioning your relationship dynamics right now and whether or not you are in a good situation. It is okay to ask these questions, and it is okay to let go of a love bond that is unhealthy for your quality of life.

Spending time with other people who have an understanding and calm nature, or who are eager to grow, reflect, and learn from their emotional experience can be a breath of fresh air to an Empath. You may not want to be with someone who is just like you and that has its own set of unique challenges. For the Empath, working on your relationships means bringing awareness and understanding to your feelings and that you are easily affected by anyone's feelings, most especially your romantic partners.

You will have to learn that shielding, balancing, grounding, and clearing are a necessary part of your romances and that you will need to find a way to help support your love experience while also supporting yourself fully.

There are other relationships that have unique challenges for the Empath, and they are familial, platonic, and professional. Take a look at the list below to see how some of these relationships can affect the Empath.

Family

- Family dynamics that force an Empath to play a certain role to make everyone else happy before their own happiness

- Obligations to parents in order to protect their feelings, even when they are making it hard for you to express yourself and your energetic truth

- Denial from parents or caregivers that you are an Empath and suggestion that you are too sensitive or that you have a condition or mental health disorder that would require special therapy or treatment

- Childhood trauma as a result of collecting and absorbing your entire family's energy, pain, or suffering

- Sensitivity to all of your own children's needs that can be very beneficial for them and you as a parent

Friends
- Imbalanced relationships with friends when you are the one who always listens and they are the one always talks

- Difficulty connecting or relating to anyone in your friend group who doesn't understand your sensitivity, causing conflict when you have certain needs or requests

- Dramatic friendships resulting in clashing attitudes and personalities when you don't want to give up your boundaries or need for your own space and time

- Empowering relationships that help you hold space for a friend's needs at all times because of your ability to respond well to their energy

Co-Workers
- Worries about being competitive with colleagues or letting others advance in their positions, because they are more aggressive

about being promoted, or because you don't want to make them feel unhappy

- Being left out or cast off because you like quiet alone time after work or on breaks, therefore, feeling ostracized by the group

- Patience and understanding with people in the office while they work, even when it is past due.

- Effective management abilities because of seeing what people are needing or sensing how they are feeling about the job.

These are certainly not all of the ways that these kinds of relationships can manifest, but the list shows a few concepts in order to present an idea of what it can be like for anyone, but specifically for an Empath.

The relationships dramas that unfold in childhood and into adulthood vary widely and are mingled with the love, happiness, and joy of being a family. If you are a person who acquires empathic skills at an early age, you may find childhood very difficult. Your parents might see you as being too sensitive and don't know why or how to answer those issues. You may be misdiagnosed with a behavioral or emotional disorder, and being an Empath falls into neither of those categories.

In childhood, you may also unconsciously choose to perform a certain role for your family, usually as the "peacemaker" or the "do-gooder" in order to help establish a balanced family dynamic, taking away from your true energy and self and forcing an identity onto you that you carry into your adult life.

You may also find that as an adult parent, your family relationships thrive because of how easy it is for you to determine what your child is needing or feeling and how you can nurture them. The best way to embrace that experience to continually guard, ground and shield your energy so that you are not exhausted after a day of childhood tantrums and skinned knees.

Friendships can be difficult if you haven't learned how to protect yourself and your energy. Some of your friendships might be more toxic than you realize and as you give yourself space to find awareness as an Empath, you may notice that some of your friendships are not good for you and are actually causing you pain or drama.

Like with all Empaths, any relationship can have its issues, and alike with a romance, friendships can experience codependency as well as an attachment to your ability to lend a shoulder to cry on or a listening ear. Empaths are easy to confide in, and for a friend who leads a life of drama, they want to be best friends with the Empath who will always permit their drama and listen to it with an open heart and mind. For the Empath, this is an incredibly taxing and unbalanced relationship that needs better boundaries and grounding.

Other situations with friends can feel incredibly rewarding, especially as you are able to offer a good council and a deep understanding of what someone is going through or celebrating. As long as the connection is balanced and you receive as much love and care in return for yours, friendship is very rewarding for the Empath and can also be rewarding to the friend who listens with equal fervor and willingness.

For many people, not just Empaths, the office is a landscape filled with little volcanoes of drama that can erupt weekly and even daily. There are a variety of personalities, expectations, goals, demands, and deadlines that make for an intensely dynamic reality. Work-related relationships are preferably professional, but sometimes, they go beyond those walls.

Anyone who has a job with coworkers knows that it can be challenging as a group or in one-on-one dynamics because everyone has their own personal career goals that they want to achieve. An Empath will be hyperaware of their colleague's energy, thoughts, expressions, and rapport throughout the workday and may feel like they need to change their own energy or work-related choices in order to accommodate other colleagues, bosses, or the whole team.

On the other hand, Empaths make excellent managers because they can look at the needs of the team or of an individual with a different set of eyes and senses and work to understand all situations a little bit better. It can be very taxing and challenging for an Empath to manage multiple personalities all day, all week, and might require an extra level of grounding and clearing at the beginning and end of the day, however, it can be very rewarding to work closely with people in your work-related relationships to help everyone thrive, as long as you are already supporting your own career ambitions.

The main point of all of this is that relationships, whether they are romantic, familial, platonic, or professional, are an important part of our life experiences. Empaths feel all of these relationships in a different way. As you decide how to help yourself grow as an Empath, you will need to take a close look at all of your close relationships and determine what energy you are experiencing within it.

Some of your relationships may feel balanced and healthy, while others may start to feel more energetically toxic and imbalanced. Using the tools and guidelines of this book to help you ground, guard, and clear your energy will help you work within your relationship dynamics in a healthier way. You will begin to notice a shift in your own energy and may look at enhancing certain relationships while letting go of others.

When you are ready to live your life embracing your gift, you will understand that the best way for you to thrive as an Empath is through awareness of what it means to live with this ability and what you will need to do to remain balanced, high in your own energy, free of other people's energy, and free to be yourself in whatever relationship you are exploring.

Chapter 7: How to Avoid Empathic Burnout

Taking the time to practice healthy boundaries, grounding and clearing practices, and different styles of meditations are a happy opening to giving you a better balance in your energy while you live as an Empath. There are a number of ways to connect to yourself and to help you align with your own internal knowing and clear energetic existence, but for some, this can feel impossible.

If you are leading a life as an Empath that is constantly putting you in situations to collect and absorb unwanted energy, then you may find yourself in an empathic burnout, exhausted, overwhelmed, and unable to reground and restabilize.

Asking yourself what people and experiences in your life are one way to start preparing yourself to avoid or prevent these moments, and in this chapter, you will find more details to help yourself attain and maintain a healthy energetic balance.

Guidelines for Maintaining Balance and Stability

As an overview from this book, the following guidelines are a quick reference and resource to keep you balanced and stable as you work and live as an Empath:

1. Practice self-awareness and mindfulness daily.

2. Create time for meditations.

3. Clear unwanted energy as often as needed with spiritual healing tools.

4. Practice grounding techniques daily.

5. Offer clear communication and necessary boundaries with people and experiences in your life.

6. Schedule quality alone time with yourself.

7. Practice self-reflection to identify issues and problems in your emotions or energy.

8. Follow a routine to help you stay protected and balanced, including the use of spiritual healing tools, meditations, and various therapies to promote stability.

9. Protect and ground yourself with the *Before and After* rule of thumb.

10. Limit time with people or groups that cause a large shift in your energy and feelings.

11. Be practical with your energy and what you intend to do; have an awareness of a situation before you walk into it to better protect yourself.

12. Value your gift as an Empath so that you are not doubtful of your abilities in the face of disrespect from others.

13. Seek out healthy relationships and partnerships rather than forcing them to work as they cause you emotional difficulty and energetic disempowerment.

14. Spend time clearing and cleansing your home as well as your body with incense, smudge sticks, and good energetic intentions.

15. Create awareness for yourself and others about what you need, rather than only serving other's needs.

Let these guidelines serve as a way to help you refresh yourself and to maintain balance and stability.

You may not need to use all of these frequently, and some you may use every day; they are excellent ways to support you on your journey and keep you aligned with your needs.

Applications to Aid You in Times of Stress or Burnout

In this section, you will find some simple steps to apply to situations that may make you feel energetically drained or stressed. Practice them to help you achieve greater stability and enjoy the results of feeling grounded even in the most stressful moments.

Affirmation Meditation

Close your eyes. Inhale and exhale deeply. Bring your attention to your feet. Feel a bright, golden light come from the floor through your feet. Let the light fill your entire body as you inhale and exhale deeply.

In your head or out loud, intone the following affirmations:

- I am comfortable in my energy, and I am grounded to the Earth.

- The golden light within me repels negative energy and protects me.

- I am able to appreciate the energy around me and not absorb it into me.

- I am aligned with only my own energy.

- I have the power to refuse another person's energy.

- I am open to other people and protected by my golden light within.

NOTE: You can change the color of the light if there is one that resonates more with you. You can also perform this affirmation meditation with your eyes open, clearly seeing and visualizing the light while you breathe and picture it flowing through you. This may come in handy at an office party or at a conference. Consider it as a good tool for your toolbox and pull it out anytime you feel a need to profess your energetic harmony and balance.

Ritual Bath for Times of Stress and Burnout

1. Find a time when you won't be disturbed by others. Silence your cell phone.

2. Draw a hot bath and add Epsom salt.

3. Light candles to bring the clearing energy of fire into the bathroom.

4. Prior to stepping into the bath, use your smudge stick (sage or other herbs) to waft the smoke around your body, clearing your auras.

5. Step into the bath and lie comfortably, submerging as much of your body as you can.

6. Soak in the salt water for at least 20 minutes and as long as 1 hour.

7. Use creative visualization to picture unwanted energy washing off of you. See yourself pulling away from anything that feels stuck to you and drops it in the water.

8. Remove your body from the bath and smudge your auras again with your herbal smudge stick.

9. Dry off and lie on your bed.

10. Meditate for 15 minutes and picture your chakras spinning clockwise, clear and open.

<u>Nature Stroll</u>

Find a serene and secluded landscape that you can quietly and calmly walk through; it may be a park in your neighborhood, or you may have to drive a little distance to find a nature reserve or a forest. Be sure to bring some water to drink and a snack of your choice.

Walk through the natural setting and soak in the energy of the landscape around you. Do not reach for your phone to take pictures or send texts to your family about where you are; just appreciate the energy of the forest, the trees, the river, the animals.

Enjoy the calmness and solace in nature for as little or as long as an hour or more. Give yourself space to enjoy an area where there are not many people. See if you can find a place that has running water, like a stream, waterfall, or riverside. Enjoy the sounds of the water flowing.

Meditate on your energy and feel the water and the trees, or any other landscape you choose, washing and blowing your cares away. Let the Earth know that you are feeling stressed and that you ask for that energy to be taken from you, and carried away. Let nature take your stress and burnout and transform it into new energy to be absorbed into the landscape.

Practice nature walking and talking as often as every week if you are prone to stress and burn out.

You can use these applications any time it feels necessary. Create awareness and involve yourself more with your energy and your own needs when it comes to refreshing yourself. The more you apply these meditations, affirmations, and other spiritual healing tools, the less you will feel weakened and burned out by people's energy.

Get creative and play! There are so many ways to take good care of yourself and your energy, and these applications and guidelines are just the beginning for how you can live your life well and happily as an Empath.

Conclusion

Being an Empath is a way for you to sense, see, and feel more of the world around you. It may feel uncomfortable for you if you don't know how to use your gift or treat it well. How you answer your calling is up to you, and you can decide all of the best ways to explore your powerful gift as someone open to more than meets the eye.

In this book, you have discovered what an Empath is and what it feels like to be someone with these qualities. You have been shown many of the common problems and realities for an Empath who is not in a healthy energy balance and who needs to spend more time taking care of their energy, as much or more as they care for others. You have discovered the gifts of being an Empath and also the kind of healing work you can do with your gift.

Taking a look at all of your skills, you can now use the chapters that outline how to guard, protect, balance, ground, and clear your energy. There are several techniques for you in this book that will help you achieve harmony with yourself while you maintain harmony with others.

Take time and make time to clear your energy using the spiritual healing tools, meditations, affirmations, applications, and guidelines in this book. Open yourself to the power of your gift and skills by taking good care of your energy and finding the freedom to live a happy and fulfilling life as an Empath! You are on the right path, and your road to discovery continues now with every step you take.

If you found this book helpful and informative, recommend it to a friend or someone you know who will benefit, and of course, you can always leave a review to help people find their road to self-discovery as an Empath.

www.ingramcontent.com/pod-product-compliance
Lightning Source LLC
Chambersburg PA
CBHW060351080526
44583CB00012B/264